even amidst horrific scandal...

Passing the Faith onto Loved Ones

How God Has Lit a Path for Catholics

Deacon John Beagan

ISBN: 9781659148015

2020

www. **Passing the Faith onto Loved Ones** .com

~

for online links to YouTube audio version,
manuscript with clickable references,
and other resources.

www. **It Makes Sense to Believe** .com

~

for those who doubt or disbelieve.

This book contains the same case and might be the one to share with loved ones. Links to YouTube audio version, and manuscript with clickable references.

to

Rose Elizabeth

CONTENTS

Rosie

Two weeks before Christmas 2019, I sent the first draft of this book to deacon classmates, priests, family members and friends for feedback. On the morning of December 20th around 6AM my son, Charlie, called me from Long Island. Crying, he said, "Dad, Rosie is dead. We're at Saint Francis Hospital. Come down right away." My son and his wife, Laura, had suddenly and unexpectedly lost their only child, our only grandchild. Rose was nearly 2 and a half years old and was perfectly healthy.

A couple of hours later, while driving through Connecticut and trying to accept the reality of what happened, my son called again. He rapidly asked two questions, "Is Rose in heaven?" and "Why did God do this?" Over the next couple of days, I heard the second question more than once.

This traumatic and tragic event tested our family's faith. And, in a sense, this book.

Rosie's last day and night were completely normal. She went to her gym class that day and was as energetic as usual. She ate a full dinner, danced around the house to music, and was exceptionally happy that night before bedtime. She had no signs of illness. As was their routine, Charlie and Laura gave her a bath, read her some stories, said prayers with her and then put her to sleep in her crib. The only difference was Rose specifically requested to say prayers on Daddy's lap – an unusual occurrence, but one Charlie treasures.

A little after midnight, Rosie woke up and Laura went in to comfort her. Rose laughed with Laura in the middle of the night, went potty, talked about going to Disney World, and rocked with Laura for a while until she was ready to go back to sleep.

Early in the morning, when Charlie got up for work, he discovered her lifeless body in her crib. They rushed to the emergency room. Although the doctors worked diligently on Rose for nearly an hour, they were unable to revive her. This was any parent's worst nightmare. Rosie was gone.

When the attempts to save Rose were over, Charlie stepped outside to call a few family members about their shocking and horrific tragedy. After he said his few words to me, a hospital security guard, who was a retired policeman, hugged Charlie like he was his father.

In the hours and days that followed, family and friends gathered in complete shock to try and comfort Laura, Charlie and each other. Their parish community, the school, their work teams, and even complete strangers, sent flowers, meals, and cards to their home.

When planning the funeral Mass at church, their pastor took Laura over to a statue of the Blessed Mother and said, "She lost a child, too." Laura remembered all the Hail Mary's she had said with Rosie before bed each night and the words, "Pray for us…now and at the hour of our death," resonated deeply. She found some peace in knowing that she was with Rose that night nearing the hour of her death.

At the funeral Mass, the church was packed. During the homily, I addressed Charlie's questions — "Was Rosie in heaven?" and "Why did God do this?"

About the first question, of course Rosie was in heaven. I baptized her in that church two years ago; she was not old enough to neglect Jesus or offend God; and she was perfectly innocent. In fact, that is clearly implied in the Church's funeral ritual for a child where in the vigil we pray, "Lord... As you washed [Rosie] in the waters of baptism and *welcomed* her into the life of heaven, so call us one day to be united with her..." There is no question where Rosie is now.

While this was a glorious situation for Rose, the trauma and devastation felt by Laura and Charlie was unbearable. How could a good God have let this happen? The second question.

On that Friday, Laura and Charlie especially, and the entire family, shared in our Lord's Passion. As our Lord's mother Mary wept at the foot of the cross and later held her son's dead body, so it was for Laura and Charlie. In fact, Charlie literally held Rose in his arms from her crib to the emergency room. Thus, December 20th was their Good Friday. Yet theirs, like Mary and Jesus, was not a pointless suffering. Rather, it was a type of witness and martyrdom.

In the biblical story of Job, Satan said to God, "The only reason Job loves you is because you have given him so many worldly blessings. Let me take away his possessions and loved ones, and he will curse you to your face." Then God allowed Satan to do his evil deeds. Later, while submerged in misery, Job proclaimed, "The Lord gives, and the Lord takes away. Blessed be the name of the Lord." (cf. Job 1)

When Rosie died, her loved ones came to a fork in the road. Should we remain faithful to God like Job, or denounce him and walk away?

Many of our Church martyrs were given a similar choice. Deny Jesus and you will not suffer and be killed. Families died while remaining faithful to the bitter end. In our tragic case, the situation was reversed. The evil was already done, and we were being asked by God to remain lovingly faithful to him. Because this is how God loves us.

I concluded my homily saying, "When our friends and colleagues see how being a practicing Catholic strengthens us in times of great adversity, they will take note, even if subconsciously. And hopefully they too will discover Jesus, the Church he established, and the divine love of God. This is His ultimate desire.

"When God pulled Rosie into heaven, he made her a saint for our family and gave her a divine purpose. Rose is praying for us so we may intentionally grow closer to God, be our Lord's witnesses on earth, and share in Jesus' saving mission. Then in the end, we will join Rosie in heaven, with all the angels and saints, in everlasting happiness, in unity with the Father, Son, and Holy Spirit, and with one another."

Yet, even with this faith, our hearts will continue to fall every time we realize Rosie is physically gone, unable to be snuggled with and enjoyed as she grows, because she was so special. Laura and Charlie in particular, will have to carry this cross every single day until they see Rosie again in heaven.

At the end of Mass, Laura's sister, Lisa, shared some words of remembrance. She called Rosie a "firecracker" with an "energetic and silly personality." Rosie had "one speed" and it was "GO." And how she loved her parents. At the end of a workday she would rock the car with excitement when she saw her parents coming off the train.

Then Lisa closed with these words:

"As everyone knows, the past few days have been profoundly heartbreaking. We are all leaning on one another and trying to process how to proceed. Fortunately for us, we need to look no further than the example that our sweet, tough and determined Rosie set for us. Rosie didn't let getting knocked down stop her. Ever. And for us, this is a massive fall. The biggest one we will ever take. But just like Rosie, we will get up and move forward. Our guardian angel will be on our shoulders, she will be in our hearts, and she will be in our actions helping us put one foot in front of the other– and eventually, we'll find that we are sprinting through the next door with a big smile on our face, spreading the same joy that she brought to us each and every day.

"Charlie and Laura have tremendous faith and they instilled that in Rose. They said prayers with her every single night. She would look forward to them and finish the verses. She went to church every single Sunday (sprinting down the aisle of course!) It's their faith and the idea of seeing Rosie again that will get Charlie and Laura through this. They have said that they have a renewed mission to get to Heaven – because that's certainly where she is and where they will be reunited.

"While our time with her was short, the time we had with her was an absolute gift from God, a blessing on this earth. We are forever fortunate and grateful that our lives were touched by such a beautiful and sweet soul. We will miss her every second of every day for the rest of our lives but know that we will see her again. May God Bless you Rosie, and may you rest in peace. We love you."

ROSIE

Two days after the funeral, at Christmas Mass, the priest during his homily said he received a photo of his 2-year-old niece earlier that morning. She was coming down the staircase and stood in awe as she stared at the extra tall, decorated Christmas tree and presents. As I listened to Father, I wondered how Laura and Charlie were receiving it. Then I thought how sad it was that Rosie could not enjoy her Christmas tree and gifts. But after a few moments I imagined what her first Christmas in heaven must be like – a scene of incomparable splendor and joy.

A week later, the old family pediatrician, who took care of Laura when she was a child, came to the house. He had spoken at length with the medical examiner and told us everything was ruled out — trauma, suffocation, fever, infection, malformed heart, etc. They concluded Rosie's heart simply stopped. There was nothing anyone could have done to prevent it or to save her. Then he referred to my homily when I had said, "It was like God reached down with both hands and pulled Rosie into heaven."

When Rose passed away, Laura was 5 months pregnant with their second child. On April 17th, just five days after Easter, in the middle of the coronavirus pandemic, Olivia Jane Beagan was born. The day before, when Laura was leaving her house to go to the hospital, she instinctively grabbed a framed picture of Rosie on her way out the door. During the delivery, Rosie's picture was on a stand directly in Laura's view. The obstetrician delivering Olivia had delivered Rose as well. As he brought Olivia into this world, he spoke to Rosie.

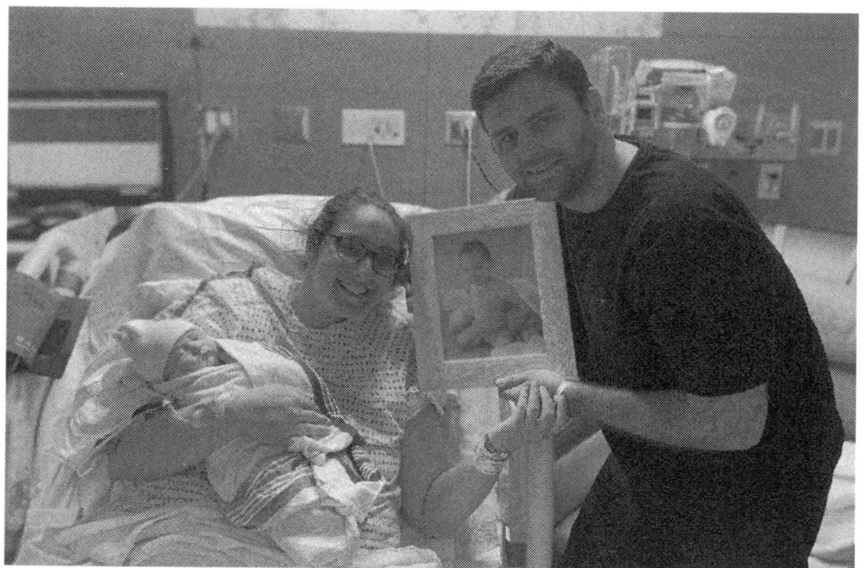

On their way home from the hospital, after first stopping by the cemetery to visit with Rose, Laura and Charlie took Olivia to church so their pastor could give her a blessing. The next day, Divine Mercy Sunday, Monsignor Clerkin offered the online Mass for Rosie and announced the birth of baby Olivia.

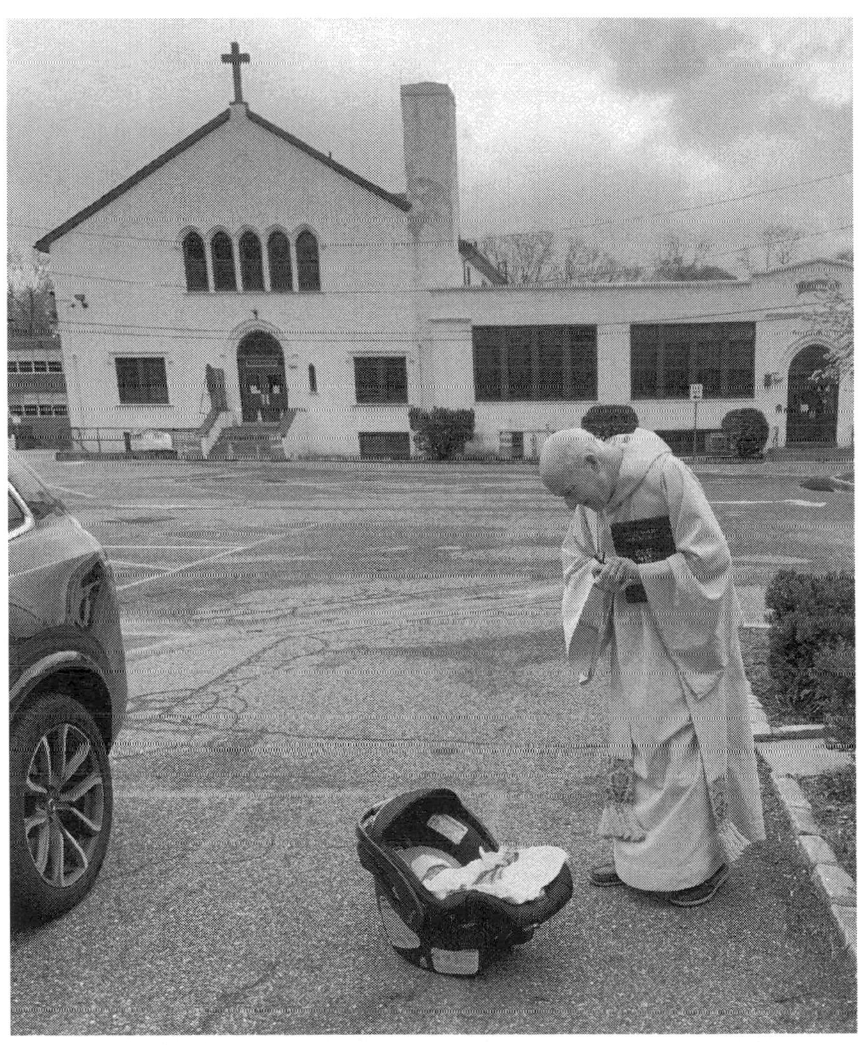

The birth of Olivia was a joyful event – an Easter Sunday that followed this family's Good Friday. Even so, every day is a kind of mix of Passion and Resurrection. There is an ever-present sadness in Rosie's physical absence – in the inability to watch her take on her role as a big sister, and in the crushing reality that their family is not the way they ever envisioned it would be at this point. But there is also joy in this new precious life that God has given to them. It is a scene of love that endures the pain.

There is no doubt as life continues, there will be waves of Passion – like when Olivia starts school, other siblings are born, and family celebrations are enjoyed. Their tears will not be completely wiped away until all of us are rejoicing together in heaven. But I do hope and trust that the blessings and joys of God will give them the strength to endure and the hope they need.

When Olivia was born, I asked Charlie what we should call her. He casually replied, "Liv... Livie... and when she's older and I'm mad, O-LIV-I-A!" Then it struck me. LIVE!

Lisa

LIV

Charlie and Laura's faith and the hope of being reunited with Rosie for eternal life has been helping them get through each day. But it's not just believing in God, Jesus, the Church, and heaven, which is crucial. It's also opening themselves to God so He may, as it says in the Psalms, "heal the brokenhearted and save the crushed in spirit." (cf. Psalms 147:3, 34:18)

When Rose passed, Charlie didn't just blindly accept his faith and assume she was in heaven. In fact, he told me how up to that moment, when he went to Mass, he was largely going through the motions. Afterwards, though, he had to know for sure where Rosie was and that they could be reunited again. So, with Laura, he launched his own investigation, reading book after book, pursuing answers to questions online, and examining the evidence, especially miracles. The more he researched, the more they became convinced this faith makes sense and is true.

Thus, on that Thursday night, it was not a coincidence they were all together, and that Charlie and Laura had their special time with Rosie. Nor was it random that the retired policeman overheard Charlie's brief call to me then hugged him with both arms. Nor was it by chance that people just showed up when Laura and Charlie needed it most, and that those with experience where available to provide guidance and support, such as priests, fellow bereaved parents, therapists, and doctors. Rather, it was God caring for them.

The reason I included this chapter was not out of some inner need to memorialize Rosie, but rather her family's passion put our faith to the test and was an example of why it's so important to be a practicing Catholic. In the wake of Rosie's passing some days are excruciatingly painful even with our strong faith. But without faith, it would be impossible.

Early in this tragic event, Charlie was struck by how sudden any of our lives can end, no matter how young and healthy we are. Now, during the coronavirus pandemic, I have been struck by how quickly vast populations can be stricken. This has intensified my concern as a father, husband, brother, uncle and deacon, to prepare loved ones who seem to have no need for God, so they may be ready when the time comes, to stand before the Father of Jesus crucified.

Saint Rosie, "Pray for us."

Introduction

This is a very difficult time to pass the Catholic faith onto loved ones, especially given the abhorrent scandals and the disbelief they engendered. Surprisingly, though, it is also perhaps the clearest of times to believe, next to standing beside Jesus during his many miracles and resurrection. Thus, this book hopes to show how God has lit a path for Catholics so they may fully believe; then, through conversation, confidently pass the faith onto those they care about and bring them back to church.

I was born in the 1950's and raised near Boston when the Church seemed to be booming. Where I grew up, a person could walk to six parishes within a mile. As a child, I remember standing in the aisle at Mass, because there were not enough seats. Then, to deal with this problem, many parishes turned their church basements into worship space so we could have two Masses at the same time.

A few years later, something started to happen. Many people stopped going to Mass; convents and Catholic schools were closed; basement worship spaces became community halls; and two of my six neighborhood parishes were shut down – each just a 5-minute walk from where I raised my children. To top it off, our Masses today are only half full. This entire precipitous decline happened just in my lifetime.

Disbelief in The Church

In the ensuing years, I have seen and read about many things leaders have done to attract people back to church and generate enthusiasm among the faithful. Despite all this good work, however, the overall trend away from Catholicism continues. According to Pew Research, for every person becoming Catholic, we are losing six.[1] This trend is even worse in the Northeast where I live, which as reported by Pew, is the least religious section in the country.[2]

Interestingly, while the rate of attrition among Catholics is much higher than all other religions, the combination of atheism, agnosticism and those unaffiliated with any religion has become the fastest growing segment.[3] The largest reason why this movement away from religion is growing so fast, is two-thirds of them did not believe what their faith professes.[4]

This is not only a major problem for former Catholics, but disbelief also affects people attending Mass. A national consulting group conducted a survey in our parish where about one third of those who come to Mass responded — presumably our most motivated. Notably, only half "strongly agreed" with Church teaching.[5]

---

[1] Pew Research (May 12, 2015) - http://www.pewforum.org/2015/05/12/americas-changing-religious-landscape/ "Nearly one-third of American adults (31.7%) say they were raised Catholic. Among that group, fully 41% no longer identify with Catholicism. This means that 12.9% of American adults are former Catholics, while just 2% of U.S. adults have converted to Catholicism from another religious tradition. No other religious group in the survey has such a lopsided ratio of losses to gains."

[2] Pew Research (Feb 29, 2016) -- https://www.pewresearch.org/fact-tank/2016/02/29/how-religious-is-your-state/

[3] Pew Research (May 12, 2015) – See above

[4] Forming Intentional Disciples, (2012) Sherry Weddell, p.32

Pew Research (Aug 8, 2018) https://www.pewresearch.org/fact-tank/2018/08/08/why-americas-nones-dont-identify-with-a-religion/

[5] In the section on personal religious belief: 52 percent did not strongly agree that the Church is critical to our relationship with God; 59 percent did not strongly agree with the teaching authority of the Church; 47 percent did not strongly agree with Jesus' moral teachings as taught by the Church; and 38 percent did not strongly agree that Scripture is the word of God.

Then a consultant explained how important it is that people "strongly agree." He said, "If you were recommending a restaurant, but only said it was OK, the person might not go and take his chances elsewhere. But if you were whole-heartedly enthusiastic, the person would probably go. And so it is when trying to pass on the faith."

Consequently, given the importance of strongly agreeing, when a Catholic picks and chooses his disputes with the Church on faith and morals, he weakens his ability to pass on the faith because he can no longer speak with enthusiasm and authority. Rather, it becomes his view in an ocean of conflicting opinion. And why should someone follow *his* assessment, even if it's one of his own adult children?

Therefore, if we want to pass the Catholic faith onto loved ones, then we must fully believe it ourselves. If we want people in the pews to passionately share the faith with others, then we must convince them how true it is. And if we want to bring many people back to church, we must convince them as well. Otherwise, we should anticipate a much smaller Church.

We should also recognize that no matter how wonderful our music is, or beautiful our church, or friendly our people, etc., the Mass cannot compete successfully against all the leisure, recreation, and entertainment options available to most people. If we only vie for people's attention on this ground, we will continue to lose the vast majority.

Admittedly, there will always be a small spirited segment of society drawn to church for various reasons. This book, however, is focused on the largest and most neglected rationale for people falling away, and that is disbelief in the Church, especially some of its teaching on faith and morals.[6]

---

[6] "We no longer believe the teachings of the Church." See Bishop Robert

But Does It Matter?

Let us pause here. Does it really matter what folks believe? Church self-interest aside, and regardless of how good church makes us feel, should we care if our loved ones choose other more enjoyable ways to spend their free time?

I am persistently troubled by one image. As our civilization increasingly neglects and forgets Jesus, how will it be as each life ends and stands before God, the father of Jesus crucified? Will that person be joyfully welcomed into heaven as almost everyone believes?

How did God the Father feel as he watched his only beloved son get tortured and crucified for hours? Are his Father's feelings still fresh today?

I had a conversation with a young public-school teacher who was raised Christian. He suggested that because Jesus was God, his crucifixion was no big deal. But the teacher forgot that Jesus emptied himself of his divinity, became fully human (Phil 2:5-8), and therefore suffered as anyone would have.

In 2007, when our 17-year-old son wanted to join the Marine Corps infantry, and fighting was still heavy, I showed him documentaries of what could happen, for instance on those who had fallen or were terribly wounded. My wife knew these discussions were happening but said nothing. When the time came and I told her she would have to sign his papers, she broke down and cried.

While I was narrowly focused on Charlie's decision, and what was right and best, Marita was imagining that one day she might

---

Barron's interview with Raymond Arroyo
https://www.youtube.com/watch?v=4ZY2oAionAU

have to, allegorically, hold her son's lifeless body in her arms and across her lap. It was her motherly reaction that later caused me to think about how God the Father felt as he watched his son hanging, nailed to a cross for hours.

Thus, given how deeply parents feel about their children, we have to ask, why did God send his only son knowing he would be killed? It had to be for a dire reason, and not just to make a speech about living a better life.

Notably, the name "Jesus" means "God saves." But saves us from what or who?

According to today's polls, many college-educated people do not believe hell exists.[7] For those who do believe, though, the risk of damnation is one of the most disturbing and controversial topics in Christianity. That is, if there is Satan and hell, then how many people go there forever, and for what reasons? And problematically, how do we reconcile everlasting horror and suffering, with God who is supposed to be love?

Yet, think about the clergy sex abuse scandals when ordained men wearing Roman collars stalked their prey, had the trust of parents and ruined their children's lives. Don't these acts cry out for divine justice? Or in the end, does everyone stroll into heaven where predators get to live next door to their victims?

In 2003, the late Jesuit Cardinal Avery Dulles, who was a well-respected theologian, wrote an article for First Things entitled, "The Population of Hell."[8] In that article, he surveyed what Jesus had to say on the matter, as well as Apostolic writings and Church teaching

---

[7] Pew Research -- https://www.pewforum.org/religious-landscape-study/educational-distribution/college/

[8] First Things -- https://www.firstthings.com/article/2003/05/the-population-of-hell

over the centuries. He observed that for the last two thousand years, until 60 years ago, Catholic theologians were in a "virtual consensus" about being concerned for people's salvation. Then there seemed to be a "break in the tradition."

Cardinal Dulles continued, "Today [there is] a kind of thoughtless optimism… Unable to grasp the rationale for eternal punishment, many Christians take it almost for granted that everyone, or practically everyone, must be saved. [They] seem to celebrate… the salvation of the deceased, without any reference to sin and punishment. More education is needed to convince people that they ought to fear God who, as Jesus taught, can punish soul and body together in hell (cf. Matthew 10:28)."

Getting People to Listen

Whether or not people's salvation is at stake, is a critical issue for promoting the faith and helping people to believe. First, if we do not uphold the reality of Satan, fallen angels and hell, for example, then renewing our baptismal promises, such as "Do you reject Satan?" will appear medieval and be another reason for people to disbelieve the Church. In other words, we uphold all God's words or we don't — people will notice.

Second and equally important, we must recognize that most people figure they have no need for God in this life or the next. Therefore, they have little or no interest in hearing anything about Jesus and the Church he founded. As middle-class Americans, we live in relatively safe and prosperous times. Practically speaking, we don't need God to be happy in this life. To the contrary, God might even interfere with our daily pleasure. Likewise, we don't need God for the next life either since almost everyone optimistically presumes eternal bliss, as Cardinal Dulles noted.

Consequently, if the Mass cannot compete with recreation and entertainment, and if we don't need God in this life or the next, then why should busy hard-working people spend invaluable free time considering Jesus and his Church?

If, however, all God's words are true, that is, official Church teaching and Sacred Scripture, and thus people's salvation is a concern, then we should be able to bring more people back to church by undermining their presumption about eternal life and taking them through our common sense reasons on why it makes so much sense to believe as a Catholic.

This bears repeating. To get people's attention so they might take all God's words to heart, we must convincingly teach that salvation cannot be taken for granted, in light of the crucifix. Like a medical professional looking for the right place to stick the needle, this is a significant entry point for those trying to pass on the faith.

The crux of my analysis, and the reason for this book and project, is that we must help our loved ones believe through evidence and reason. To get their attention, we must undermine their presumption about eternal life. If, however, we continue to passively watch people get unnecessarily swallowed up by various doubts, then we will continue to shrink as a Church until we become a faithful remnant. And this will happen despite our energetic preoccupation with daily responsibilities, creative programs, and best practices.

Depressingly, some bishops and pastors have already resigned themselves to becoming a remnant. But I wouldn't give up, especially if we haven't been promoting all God's words.

It pains me as a deacon to face the pews, look at the large number of empty seats, and worry about the people outside church not preparing to meet God. Yet, one of the things that bewilders me most is that many fully believing Catholic preachers and teachers treat the reality of Satan, hell and judgement as a topic reserved for advanced members. But isn't this like standing on the side of a fast moving, busy road, where people are racing in the dark toward a bridge with a big hole in it, and not at least holding up a lit warning sign? Isn't it our Christian obligation and an act of spiritual mercy to try to alert people as the Catechism warns us? (CCC 1852)

I don't know why instructors of the faith avoid warning people. Are they afraid to upset folks? Do they need to be popular and liked? Are they worried for their jobs?

When will these evangelists get tired of losing? And how will they explain to God the Father that they could only promote *some* of His Son's words?

At various points over the years, my grown sons have gone off-road. However, I never discounted God's words because my loved ones weren't living up to them. Instead, I patiently upheld all Church teaching and invisible realities, and prayed they would get back on track.

As a dad, I could never let my children go astray without occasionally and directly bringing it to their attention. I love them and God too much to watch passively. Likewise, as an ordained deacon, I have to care for all my brothers and sisters as I do my own family.

The Drama of Salvation

Bishop Robert Barron is one of the most extraordinary teachers and preachers of the Catholic faith in the United States. However, if you are familiar with his approach to evangelization, then you realize I am out of sync with his method for engaging people and bringing them back to Mass. Bishop Barron recommends leading with what is beautiful about the Church, such as art, architecture and music; then following with what is good, such as Mother Theresa; and ending with what is true about faith and morals.

As I stated earlier, I don't think beautiful churches, etc., will get many of today's busy people to cancel their golf outing or day at the beach to go to Mass. I'm just being practical. Rather, I recommend leading with the risk of salvation, followed by truth, goodness, beauty and controversial teachings.

I must also disagree with Bishop Barron on another important, but related point – that it is reasonable to hope everyone is saved and thus hell might be empty. While I pray regularly for everyone's salvation, I do not expect it, nor would I want my children to relax on this point. Rather, I choose to stay close to all God's words as actually written, and not to wishful imaginings.

Incidentally, there was an online exchange[9] between Professor Ralph Martin and Father Robert Barron over Professor Martin's book, Will Many Be Saved? Interestingly, this debate is similar to the one Cardinal Dulles describes in his article[10] between Catholic

---

[9] https://www.catholicnewsagency.com/column/how-many-are-saved-2383

https://www.renewalministries.net/wordpress/comments-by-dr-ralph-martin-on-fr-robert-barrons-review-of-will-many-be-saved/

[10] First Things -- https://www.firstthings.com/article/2003/05/the-population-of-hell

editors, Father Richard John Neuhaus and Dale Vree.

The debate about whether hell is empty, is theologically sophisticated and nuanced. Nevertheless, we must take a position. Will we stay close to Jesus' actual words, those of his Apostles and official Church teaching? Or will we adhere to a popular sentiment that follows a position of Father Hans Urs von Balthasar as expressed by Bishop Barron when he said:

> I take the Balthasar view... that it's legitimate to hope for universal salvation. Further, it's a reasonable hope. It's not just a hope against hope, a wild, unwarranted move. Rather, it's grounded in what Christ accomplished on the Cross and in the resurrection.[11]

Cardinal Dulles, however, while recognizing Balthasar's view as being technically "orthodox," added:

> Balthasar's position... is at least adventurous. It runs against the obvious interpretation of the words of Jesus in the New Testament and against the dominant theological opinion down through the centuries, which maintains that some, and in fact very many, are lost.[12]

While I am not taking a firm position as to how many people are in hell, I am asserting that this is a very real and dire risk – if we take Jesus' words seriously. As I will explain by the end of this book, the position we choose to take in this subtle debate has enormous implications. In fact, the future of the Church and world greatly hinges on whether we think salvation is a serious ongoing issue.

---

[11] To Light A Fire On The Earth, 2017, Robert Barron with John L. Allen, Jr., p.177

[12] First Things -- https://www.firstthings.com/article/2003/05/the-population-of-hell

"Your Servant Is Ready"

We live in a time when it is truly easy to receive God's mercy. All we have to do is turn away from sin, attend Sunday Mass, regularly take God's words to heart and go to confession. Then when our last moment on earth comes, we will be able to pray with confidence as Simeon did when he held the baby Jesus in the Temple, "Lord, now your servant is ready to go to you in peace." (Luke 2:29)

The goal of this book is to help caring Catholics have conversations with loved ones; guide them through why it makes so much sense to believe as the Church does despite grievous scandals, unpopular moral positions, the controversial role of women, and a confusing array of religious beliefs in this world; and most importantly, prepare them to stand before God, the father of Jesus crucified.

This brief book is a simple, reasoned case[13] amid a climate of doubt and disbelief. It is a distillation from an average guy who has spent many years pursuing answers to faith's questions and challenges, then trying to pass this understanding on to loved ones and fellow parishioners. In a practical orderly way, this book tries to walk people through the evidence and why it makes so much sense to believe in God, Jesus and his Church.

As you'll see in a moment, the approach used throughout this case will emphasize the importance of truth. Next, will proceed with the big picture, such as, "Does God Exist?" Then, we'll zoom in to consider Christianity and the Catholic Church vis-a-vis many religious options. Finally, with this context in mind, we will deal with

[13] Other authors have written books making a case for the Catholic faith and listing reasons why it makes sense to believe. These authors include Trent Horn, Jimmy Akin, Peter Kreeft and Brandon Vogt.

controversial issues, such as scandals, sexual morality and the role of women. At the end of the case, we'll conclude with a chapter on having faith conversations as well as a few related thoughts on evangelization, preaching, teaching and vocations.

Parish Outreach

Church as "field hospital" is a beautiful image of people coming to Mass for healing and peace. And some rightly come to church for this reason. But "church as field hospital" can also be a misleading and passive image. The fact is, in middle-class America, most people are basically healthy, both physically and financially, and therefore fully capable of contributing to parish life and actively spreading the faith if they choose.

There has been some emphasis by parishes to reach out to people in their geographic area. But this is difficult to do in terms of time, money and success because little or no trusting relationship has been established between the parish and those they're trying to reach.

Alternatively, since loved ones often live apart in different parishes, if we as a broader Church were able to motivate and equip parishioners to have faithful conversations with those whom they love, no matter where they live, then all parishes would benefit.

At the very least, though, may those who read this book bring their loved ones closer to Jesus and his Church through the grace and mercy of God.

The Importance of Truth

So here we are with those we care most about, on the conveyor belt of this short life, where we got on at birth and will step off at death, and we need to make a decision about God, Jesus and the Catholic Church.

Does God *really* exist? And if so, is Jesus who he said he was, son of the living God who came to save us for love, and from sin and eternal punishment? More, is the Catholic Church the *one* church he established to guide, nourish, and inspire us along the way?

We cannot base this important decision simply on our imagination, feelings, and intuition. As people who live in an era of emotion fueled by entertainment, mass media, social media and misinformation, we must intentionally think using the best information available.

For instance, suppose you were about to drive alone to visit an old friend in some remote, far away location, where you've never been, like Richland, Washington. Would you just jump in the car and go without a GPS, using only your intuition to get there?

In any decision that will significantly affect our lives, we need true guidance more than wishful thinking. This also applies to our decision about God, Jesus and his Church; and is especially important if we are responsible for guiding children and influencing grandchildren.

Pursuing truth and what is most likely true is key to making this faith decision. In fact, Jesus said, "…the truth will make you free." (John 8:32)

Truth first became important to me when I was 9 years old. At the time, I was a compulsive liar. I remember my mother asking me a question, then as I walked away, I thought, "I'm lying even when I don't have to." One night, I had a dream that changed my life. In the dream I remembered being in the backseat of the family car, and every time we passed the stone statue of an angel, I would look up and see it smiling at me. This time, however, the angel frowned. I instantly awoke, frightened to my core. From that moment, I was committed to always tell the truth even if I would get in trouble. Then gradually over the years, I noticed how important it is to tell the truth and face reality.

For instance, consider the importance of truth in day-to-day life:

- Judges and juries need honest information to send the right people to prison.
- If we could not rely upon the rules, constants and facts of math, science and engineering, then bridges and tall buildings would collapse; planes would fall from the sky; and medicines would be ineffective or harmful.
- How would you feel if a doctor lied to you about needing immediate surgery?
- And we must be careful not to be misled and emotionally manipulated by advertising and sales professionals.

While truth is essential in life, very often we must make significant decisions without complete information – that is, when we don't know all the facts, details and nuance. Keep in mind, though, choosing to make no decision is still a decision.

As already stated, but worth repeating, no matter how strongly we believe or imagine or feel about something, will not make it real and true. Strong feelings and intuition will not get us to Richland, Washington.

I remember teaching an 8th grade Sunday school class alongside a busy 4-lane street. When I tried to emphasize the importance of reality and truth over strong feelings and imagination, a student disagreed with me. So, I asked her, "You mean if you stand in the middle of a lane in that street, with a truck racing toward you, and you strongly imagine the truck isn't there, it will not be there?"

She said, "Yeah."

I'm sure that student was grounded enough in reality to not stand in front of an oncoming truck. But the disconnect with her words bothered me and seemed to be indicative of what I currently see in distorted political discourse and biased news. Saint Luke's Gospel warns us about ignoring reality and truth. "[God] scattered [them] in the imagination of their hearts." (Luke 1:51)

To avoid getting lost in our imaginary world, we must be radically and absolutely committed to truth and reality, and not misled by our own imaginings or fancies of others. We must collect the facts and consider them. Then, even without perfect knowledge, make the best decision. Imagination and intuition have a role to play, but they are subordinate to knowledge.

In the next few sections, we're going to see how likely it is that God exists. Then in a spirit of humility, we will try to determine if God revealed himself to us. And if God did reveal himself, was it through Jesus Christ and his Catholic Church?

Does God Most Likely Exist?

Let's consider three topics – the Big Bang; the mathematical odds that the universe can exist as it is right now; and human appreciation for beauty.

The BIG BANG

One day, while I drove to the high school to pick up my teenagers, I was listening to Science Friday on National Public Radio. The program featured two scientists discussing the origin of the universe. One scientist said something like, "At the moment of the Big Bang, almost 14 billion years ago, space, matter and time started." His statement surprised me because I had never thought of "time" beginning with the Big Bang.

Now imagine you are a scientist who fully believes in a material explanation for everything, i.e., all things have a scientific cause and explanation even if we don't fully understand it, yet. Consider the traumatic implications when trying to ponder the moment before the Big Bang and you realize that science, looking into the past, ends at the Bang.

That is, a scientist looking for what preceded and caused the Big Bang sees ABSOLUTELY NOTHING – No time, no space, no material – NOTHING.

Physicist Robert Jastrow wrote in, <u>God and the Astronomers,</u> p.107, "… science [may] never be able to raise the curtain on the mystery of creation. For the scientist who has lived by his faith in the power of reason, the story ends like a bad dream.

Geneticist, Francis Collins, who headed the Human Genome

Project, wrote in his book, The Language of God, p.67, "The Big Bang cries out for a human explanation. It forces the conclusion that nature had a defined beginning. I cannot see how nature could have created itself. Only a supernatural force that is outside of space and time could have done that."

What Are the Odds?

In 2003, I browsed through my oldest son's 10th grade biology book. It asserted life as we know it came about by an accumulation of errors, i.e., by chance or luck. During this process, the book stated, "most scientists" believe conditions were such on primitive earth that inanimate molecules mixed with energy, such as ultraviolet radiation, and produced the first living cells. Then the textbook laid out a chance and material explanation for life, barely hinting at any large scientific unknowns.

Therefore, it's worth considering, "What are the odds that the planet earth and universe, in all its detail, exist at this moment?"

First, let us consider the size of the universe and all the matter it contains, as well as how tiny matter can be. Then let's calculate the odds that this moment exists.

We live in an expanding universe where everything is in motion. It contains billions of galaxies, and each galaxy has billions of stars like our sun, presumably with planets in orbit. The distance between galaxies is measured in light years, or increments of 6 trillion miles, which is the span light can travel in one year. The average distance between galaxies is 3 million light years. That means, if you could travel at the speed of light, it would take 3 million years, on average, to get to the next galaxy. The enormity of space boggles the mind.

Now consider all the material in the universe – solid, liquid, gas, etc., and how tiny it is. All matter is comprised of very small atoms.

Each atom has a nucleus and at least one electron whirling about it in an orbital. Its nucleus contains almost all an atom's mass, but only a tiny fraction of its space. If an atom were magnified to the size of a football stadium, its nucleus would be about the size of a grape and its outermost electrons would be in the highest bleachers. In other words, an atom contains mostly space.

So, let's calculate the odds by arbitrarily starting at one billion years ago, that in one freeze-frame moment long after the Big Bang, every nucleus and electron will be in that precise 3-dimensional location. Since this probability is incalculable, given all the matter, space and possibilities, let's simply conclude it is very impossible.

Now, the real interesting thing about calculating the probability that one event will happen after another, is you *multiply* each probability. So, as everything in the universe moves, the probability that one freeze-frame moment will follow the next would be impossible times impossible and so forth. Considering all the moments in the past one billion years, not to mention the previous 13 billion, our current moment is COMPLETELY impossible.

Some, however, will say, "The fact we're here is all we need to know." But that overlooks the obvious point that every moment is impossible. When we stop to really think about this, every moment is a kind of miracle.

Therefore, in contrast to my son's textbook, it is totally impossible that the universe can exist from a random cause.

And let me add, there is a complex host of factors that provide the correct balance for the rich diversity of life on earth, such as, the right intensity of the sun, our distance from it, the size and proximity of the moon, our location in the galaxy, and so forth. What are the odds of this, too, and that the cycle of nature should function so well?

And what about intricate human systems such as vision, hearing, and brain processes that they should operate with such reliability and precision? Are we to conclude all these can be attributed to luck?

Beauty

How do we reconcile mankind's appreciation for beauty, like flowers, birds, art and music, with evolution and Darwin's survival of the fittest? If anything, stopping to ponder or create beauty interferes with doing the things necessary to survive and win. So where does mankind's appreciation of beauty come from? If it comes from evolution, it was a bad mistake. If it comes from God, then we have a lot to look forward to in heaven.

Quite Possibly, There Is a God

So, given the overwhelming evidence…

- That all time, space and matter began almost 14 billion years ago, and before that moment, there was absolutely nothing;
- That it is outrageously impossible for all material and life to happen by error or chance;
- That our universe, galaxy, solar system and planet are precisely ordered to cause life to flourish on earth;
- And that survival of the fittest does not explain man's appreciation for beauty...

Isn't it quite possibly true there is a Creator God who made everything that is visible and invisible?

Now we can believe in alternatives like, parallel universes, for which there is no evidence. But that would take at least as big a leap of faith as believing in God. Therefore, doesn't it make sense to consider God might exist especially if there is evidence?

Thus, as we pursue what is most likely true let us suppose God exists; examine evidence for the Catholic faith in relation to other beliefs; and finally check if it all makes sense and ties together. Before we do this, however, let's consider the decision to practice no religion.

The Unreligious

As mentioned in the introduction, according to Pew Research, atheism, agnosticism and having no religion are becoming more popular. Some of them advocate a material-only explanation for the universe. But this is highly unlikely based on the Big Bang and mathematical probability.

I have an atheist friend who seems to lean toward scientism. He *believes* that science will one-day answer all our questions about the vast universe, like about the origin of the Big Bang. However, this is simply a huge leap of faith in the power of people with 3-pound brains.

Secularism or an areligious culture, on the other hand, seems to believe in everything and nothing. That is, all religious beliefs are equally true and untrue, and that there is no authoritative body of divine truth that we can count on. Secularism is mostly what we're testing in this book, which is, did God reveal and preserve his truth or not?

Aliens

Since we have been considering the universe, we should look at people's belief in intelligent extraterrestrial life. Now I thoroughly enjoy watching movies with aliens. But after seeing so many of these films, we might start to believe they really exist. And if our religion does not seem to be scientifically current enough to accommodate aliens, we might begin to lose faith and conviction.

According to Newsweek Magazine (9/29/2015), YouGov, one of Britain's most reputable pollsters (BusinessInsider.com), reports that most people in America believe intelligent alien life exists.

But before our faith weakens, we must observe, there is simply no evidence for alien life, especially super-advanced alien civilizations that travel here from distant galaxies and planets.

The sheer distance between galaxies, and between stars within galaxies makes it unlikely that aliens, even if they exist, could travel to our planet. To date, it seems theoretically we cannot make anything that travels faster than the speed of light. The nearest galaxy to us is 2 million light years away. The nearest star is 4 light years away. Creating material spaceships that can transport material beings those distances in reasonable amounts of time might never be possible.

I remember a popular scientist on educational TV saying, "How arrogant we must be to presume we are the only intelligent life in the universe." But consider this question: What is more arrogant – to believe we are the only intelligent life in the universe or that the one true God gave us on earth his only beloved son?

I would not let the idea of intelligent alien life disturb our faith, mostly because of a lack of evidence, but also the improbability that they could travel to earth due to vast distances. Moreover, creation took no effort for the all-powerful God. So, he could have made the entire universe just for earthlings without breaking a sweat. Remember, God simply spoke, and it was made. (Genesis chapter 1)

Humility & Mystery

As we suppose the existence of God in our analysis, the creator of the universe and all that is seen and unseen, let us humbly recognize that we have small brains. In the eyes of the universe, these are not even specks of organic dust. Therefore, if the Creator reveals knowledge to us, we must humbly leave room for mystery, because mystery is the difference between what the Creator knows and what we with tiny brains know.

We must also be open to the possibility of invisible realities – like heaven and hell, angels and demons – and to supernatural miracles and diabolic activity. In other words, spiritual beings with supernatural power might exist.

Did God Reveal Himself? 12 Criteria

Are There Many Ladders to Heaven?

We live in a time when 40% of people who were baptized Catholic,[14] have decided to leave the faith, presumably for other religious or secular beliefs. When I was a student in public high school, our history teacher, who was a very kind and caring man about the same age as my parents, said, "there are many ladders to heaven," implying it really doesn't matter what you believe. In our age of tolerance, this is a very popular position. But while we would all like to believe it, does it actually make sense in light of the crucifixion?

Now, we must presume truth is important to God because it is so important to us, his creation. However, there is a multitude of religions whose major doctrines conflict with one another. Further, it is unreasonable God would scatter his truth among many different faiths without giving us the ability to know for sure what is true and not true. Else, why give us truth at all?

Moreover, from a Christian perspective, it is also unreasonable God would send his only beloved son to us, knowing he would be crucified, just to tell us there are many ladders to heaven and it doesn't matter which one you climb because everyone gets to the same place. Therefore, if God wanted to reveal himself clearly, and

[14] Pew Research study (May 12, 2015) -- Nearly one-third of American adults (31.7%) say they were raised Catholic. Among that group, fully 41% no longer identify with Catholicism. http://www.pewforum.org/2015/05/12/americas-changing-religious-landscape/

since there is no divine key to identify what's true in every faith, then he must have done it through only one religion.

In the body of this book, I'm going to use 12 criteria to evaluate Catholicism with occasional comparisons to other major faiths. These criteria, in my opinion, should be satisfactorily met by the one true religion that comes from God.

Please note, however, in referring to other religions, I intend no disrespect to those who adhere to various faiths. In fact, since I work in the technology sector and live near Boston, I have many colleagues, friends and neighbors who believe all kinds of things. That said, however, since all religions disagree on various significant points, and cannot all be completely true at the same time, then only one can possess the fullness of divine truth.

#1 - Revelation

If God were visible, we would not be having this discussion about whether or not he exists. Since God is invisible, however, then God must reveal himself. Otherwise we have no way to know him. Therefore, revelation is our 1st essential criterion.

Interestingly, Buddhism does not believe in divine revelation and in a personal creator, God, that interacts with humanity. In fact, it does not believe in the beginning of creation either which contradicts the Big Bang.

In contrast, the Catholic Church believes God did create all that is visible and invisible out of nothing. Of course, the visible part is consistent with the Big Bang. The Church also believes God has revealed himself to humanity through Sacred Scripture, Sacred Tradition, and through the Church's central teaching authority, also known as the Magisterium.

An invisible God, however, raises a series of questions. If God exists, then why did he create us? If he wants us to know him, then why remain invisible? We will address these questions soon when we consider "love." Before that, though, let's look at a few more criteria used in this analysis.

#2 - The Words of God

The Catholic Church believes the Bible, i.e., Sacred Scripture, is the divinely inspired recording of God's revelation to mankind from the beginning of creation to its culmination in Jesus Christ. God's revelation also comes to us through the Church's ongoing and traditional understanding of God's words. Consequently, if the Bible is entirely inspired by God, then the teaching of the Catholic Church must be a reasonable interpretation of Sacred Scripture. Likewise, the 73 documents of the Bible, written over thousands of years by many divinely inspired authors must be internally consistent since all of Sacred Scripture is authored by God and truly the Word of God. (cf. CCC 132-141)

Therefore, the reasonableness and consistency of Scripture and Church teaching over time is the 2nd criterion that must be met.

The Bible

For hundreds of years, the Bible has come under great scrutiny. This can be a good thing, for instance, as we try to understand the historical and archeological context in which these documents were created. But I often cannot help suspecting that many people want to make names for themselves, or be part of the faculty club that wants to discredit the Bible, by judging parts of it as fiction or errant. Then around every Christmas and Easter, the media trots out these "scholars," so the average person does not know what to believe. Usually, the media pits fundamentalist interpretation against doubting scholars, and not a more careful Catholic understanding.

Let me share with you several brief reasons why I believe all the words in Sacred Scripture are inspired by God.

- When the Bible is properly understood within its ancient context, languages, and literary genre, it is possible for God that all these words are true.
- Given our significant distance from ancient history and scarcity of relevant data, it is impossible to disprove Biblical accounts.
- The Catholic Church teaches, "Through all the words of Sacred Scripture, God speaks only one single Word… For this reason, the Church has always venerated the Scriptures as she venerates the Lord's Body. She never ceases to present to the faithful the bread of life, taken from the one table of God's Word and Christ's Body." (CCC 102-103)
- Nowhere does the Church teach that the Bible contains errors. To the contrary, Pope Pius XII taught, "…as the substantial Word of God became like to men in all things, 'except sin,' so the words of God, expressed in human language, are made like to human speech in every respect, except error." (Pope Pius XII, Divino Afflante Spiritu, 37)
- Therefore, since the Church likens Scripture to the Eucharist and Incarnation, I ask if one believes the consecrated bread is the body of Christ, though science would certainly see it differently, why not also believe in all the words of the Word Made Flesh? (cf. John 1:14)
- God designed us to appreciate true stories. This is why marketers of new books and movies never hesitate to announce something is based on a true story or inspired by a true story. Likewise, news programs and reality shows are very popular.

Since God wired us to enjoy true stories, it makes little sense that the Bible should be fiction.

- Jesus referred to the Old Testament many times, including two of the biggest "fish stories" in Scripture, Jonah and Noah, while making two significant predictions about himself – his Resurrection and Second Coming.

  Regarding his resurrection, Jesus said, "As Jonah was three days and three nights in the belly of the whale, so will the Son of man be three days and three nights in the heart of the earth." (Matthew 12:40)

  Then about his second coming, Jesus said, "As were the days of Noah, so will be the coming of the Son of man." (Matthew 24:37)

Again, isn't it possible for God that these stories can be true? So, should I place my trust in the words of Jesus, who is the Word of God made flesh (John 1:1,14) or in people who doubt his words?

While the Catholic Church has not declared whether the stories of Jonah and Noah are more fact than fiction, I personally choose to believe them.[15,16] In the case of Noah, for instance, maybe the flood pertained to all the land the author knew about.

My concern about calling things fiction or errant, is we might miss a deeper message from God. But I see no downside to trying to carefully understand and believe.

Interestingly, in the beginning of the Bible when Satan was tempting Adam and Eve, the first few words out of the devil's

---

[15] re. Jonah, see https://www.catholic.com/qa/is-the-story-of-jonah-and-the-whale-a-myth

[16] re. Noah, see https://www.catholic.com/magazine/online-edition/a-catholic-perspective-on-a-new-attraction

mouth were, "Did God **really** say…?" (Genesis 3:1) So, the first temptation which led to the fall of humankind began with, "Did God **really** say…?" – words from the Deceiver that caused us to doubt God's words.

Judaism & Protestant Christianity

Both Judaism and Protestant Christianity mostly use the same Scriptures as Catholicism. Of course, Judaism only uses the Old Testament. Therefore, since the Bible is God's words, then we must consider the reasonableness of these faiths according to all of Scripture. We'll look first at Judaism and how things changed for their faith after Christ's death. After the next criterion on central authority, we will consider Protestant Christianity in a similar way.

Judaism

The Bible is divided in two parts, the Old and New Testaments. The Old Testament is a major element of the Jewish faith in which their history and relationship with God is recorded. The first 5 books of the Bible are attributed to Moses even though the first book, Genesis, was possibly handed down through oral history, at least in part.

The second book, Exodus, describes how Moses led his people out of slavery in Egypt through the power of God about 1300 years before Christ. During that time, God prescribed many religious observances and worship practices, including animal sacrifice in the "temple." Initially, the "temple" was a tent-like, portable sanctuary called the "tabernacle," the place where God dwelled with his chosen people.

Three hundred years later, about 1000 years before Christ, King Solomon replaced the tent with a huge stone temple in Jerusalem, a permanent place for God to dwell among his people.

From Moses to Christ, about 1300 years, the Jewish people had a very rich spiritual history with prophets, additions to Sacred Scripture, a temple, and prescribed animal sacrifices.

However, since the time of Christ, almost 2000 years ago, the Jewish people have not had their temple in Jerusalem; and they have not had new prophets and additions to Scripture. Further, God's promise to send them a Messiah has not been fulfilled.

If I were a religious Jew who pursued truth and wanted to believe Scripture, I would feel compelled to investigate and see if Jesus might be the Messiah and fulfillment of Old Testament promises (Luke 24:27b). Otherwise, given God's apparent inactivity in the past two millennia, I would tend to doubt Scripture.

I suppose a Jewish person could say to a Christian, "But it's 2000 years and Jesus hasn't returned either." Which is true. But there is an enormous difference in Judaism before and after 70 A.D. when the temple was destroyed by Rome. In contrast, Jesus said only God the Father knows the time when he will come again, meanwhile go out to the whole world, baptize and celebrate the Eucharist in memory of me. Since, Jesus' death and resurrection, and the descent of the Holy Spirit, the Catholic Church has done exactly that. While this is not proof, it is a weighty consideration.

#3 - Central Authority

This takes us to the 3rd criterion – central authority. As we have many religions that disagree with each other, so within each religion we have factions and individuals that disagree. This is because people inherently see things differently. Not only that, they might adopt contrarian positions for personal gain. For instance, I went to a training for consultants where the instructor, who was a successful businessman, said we would have to be contrarian if we want to make a name for ourselves.

Therefore, given how people naturally disagree, the religion that God reveals himself through must have a strong, divinely appointed, central teaching authority. As mentioned earlier, the Catholic Church has this in its Magisterium. However, few major religions have a central teaching authority. In fact, the only other one I can think of is the Mormon Church, formally known as The Church of Jesus Christ of Latter-day Saints.

I will refer to the Mormon Church a few more times in this book, so let me describe it briefly. This is an American born religion that was founded in the early 1800's by Joseph Smith. Since then it has been growing around the world. It is not a "Christian" church in the sense that their Book of Mormon supersedes the Bible and they have a different view of who Jesus is. In structure, it has curious similarities to the Catholic Church. For instance, their temples correspond to Catholic cathedrals; they also have priests and apostles; and their prophet is analogous to the pope, except the Mormon prophet receives divine revelation.

Central divine authority is perhaps the most difficult criteria for people to accept because it makes us tangibly accountable to the Church and God. Yet, this is how God set things up in Catholicism.

Jesus did not want a fragmented Church with contradicting leadership. Rather, he wanted a unified Church. Shortly before his arrest Jesus prayed for his disciples saying, "…Holy Father …may they be one, even as we are one." (John 17:11)

And Jesus said to them, "A new commandment I give to you, that you love one another; even as I have loved you… By this all men will know that you are my disciples, if you have love for one another." (John 13:34)

Jesus knew he had to be crucified and leave his disciples, so he told them, "I will not leave you orphans…" (John 14:18) "…the Holy Spirit, whom the Father will send in my name, he will teach you all things, and bring to your remembrance all that I have said to you." (John 14:26)

Jesus knew his Church would need central leadership, so he renamed his Apostle, Simon, to Peter, which means "rock," and said to him, "… you are Peter, and on this rock I will build my church, and the powers of death will not prevail against it." (Matthew 16:18-19)

Calling Simon "Rock" was a powerful image because Jesus himself is the rock used throughout Scripture and is the "cornerstone" that the "builders rejected." (Matthew 21:42)

Then Jesus said to Simon now called Peter, "I will give you the keys of the kingdom of heaven, and whatever you bind on earth will be bound in heaven, and whatever you loose on earth will be loosed in heaven." (Matthew 16:18-19)

Think about it. This was tremendous authority Jesus gave Peter, "…**whatever** you bind on earth will be bound in heaven, and **whatever** you loose on earth will be loosed in heaven."

Jesus further commissioned Peter when he said, "…Feed my lambs. …Tend my sheep. [and] …Feed my sheep." (John 21:15-17)

Jesus established one Church and made Peter its head. The Pope, who sits in the Seat of Saint Peter, assumes the authority of Christ on earth, especially when he teaches on faith and morals.

Jesus assured his apostles, "The Holy Spirit will come and teach you all things." Then before sending his disciples ahead to proclaim, "The kingdom of God is near you," Jesus said to them, "…He who hears you hears me…" (Luke 10:1-16)

Given Jesus' words, we can and should fully trust the teaching of the Catholic Church on faith and morals.

Now, while the Holy Spirit protects the central authority of the

Church from teaching error, the Holy Spirit does not protect members of the Church, no matter how high or low in rank, from committing egregious sin and scandal – a situation we are horribly aware of today.

That said, however, we must remember that even Jesus had Judas. Moreover, Jesus foresaw that the Church would have wolves in sheep's clothing (cf. Matthew 7:15) and that weeds would grow with the wheat until the end of time when the weeds would be gathered and burned. (cf. Matthew 13:24-30)

We must also recognize, in our morally weakened condition within a world of temptation, that everyone in the Church, including ourselves, is capable of serious sin. Remember how King David loved God, but also took Uriah's wife, Bathsheba, then had him killed.

Protestantism

Protestantism began about 500 years ago in Germany when Martin Luther, aided by some secular German rulers, successfully broke away from the Catholic Church and started his own following. Up to that point, there was only one Christian church in Western civilization, except for the largely political and cultural split between the Church in Rome and Eastern Orthodoxy of Constantinople about the year 1000. Martin Luther was soon mimicked in other parts of Europe by King Henry VIII, Ulrich Zwingli, John Calvin, John Smyth, and John Wesley.

Instead of "reforming" the Church as many history textbooks suggest by using the term "Protestant Reformation," this situation shattered the Church so that today we have thousands or tens of thousands of separate Christian denominations and independent churches – even churches of one person, where an individual reads the Bible alone, prays by himself, and is not affiliated with any

Christian community. Thus, in hindsight, a more precise term might be Protestant "De-unification."

The most significant "pillar of authority" for Martin Luther and most Protestant churches, especially Evangelical and Fundamentalist, is the Bible. Ironically, however, Scripture does not say that about itself. Here is what the Bible says about the Bible:

In the Gospels, Jesus taught and argued from Scripture many times. In one instance while buttressing his argument, Jesus asserted, "...Scripture cannot be broken..." (John 10:35)

Saint Paul wrote to Timothy, "All scripture is inspired by God and profitable for teaching, reproof, correction, and training in righteousness..." (2 Timothy 3:16)

But Paul also wrote Timothy, "... the household of God, which is the church of the living God, [is] the pillar and bulwark of the truth." (1 Timothy 3:15) Saint Paul called the *Church* "the pillar and bulwark of truth," not Scripture.

This is entirely consistent with history. Jesus, himself, did not write a single word. After his disciples received the Holy Spirit at Pentecost, they didn't sit down, write the New Testament and then go preaching. No, they probably taught for many years and occasionally wrote letters, before sitting down to write an orderly account of Christ's life, death and resurrection. Afterward, in the late 4th century, it was the Church that officially decided which ancient documents were inspired by God and would be included in Sacred Scripture, and which were to be excluded.

Therefore, the Protestant claim that Scripture and not the Church is the pillar of authority, is not supported by Scripture itself, nor history. Also, due to its enormous fracturing, Protestantism does not satisfy the criterion of central authority.

#4 - Consistently True

The 4th criterion pertains to truth. In particular, what was once true is always true.

As just mentioned, Christ established the Seat of Peter, the papacy. The pope and all the bishops teaching in communion with him comprise the teaching authority of the Church, the Magisterium. By the power of the Holy Spirit, the teaching authority is inspired and protected against error. (John 14:26) For us, it means we can completely trust the teaching of the Church on faith and morals. This teaching is most conveniently summarized in the Catechism of the Catholic Church which, incidentally, heavily footnotes Sacred Scripture. In fact, Scripture is the "very soul" of Church theology (CCC 132)

Interestingly, in the middle ages during the height of wealth, power and scandal in the Roman Catholic Church, the Magisterium never blatantly taught error. That is, the Church never changed her mind on a traditional teaching. Religious practices and disciplines changed. Teaching was reformulated and refined. But what was once true, was always true.

This is in contrast to Mormonism, for instance. The head of the Mormon church, their prophet, can declare at any time that God has revealed something to him. So, in the mid 1800's he declared polygamy was mandated by God, but in 1890 a subsequent prophet reversed this revelation when Utah was applying for statehood. This begs the question, in the eyes of God is polygamy good or not? Or does God change his mind?

Another example concerned the Mormon position about people of color. The Book of Mormon talks about Jews emigrating to South America hundreds of years before Christ. However, they were attacked by the Lamanites. As punishment God cursed the

Lamanites with "dark skin." Probably for this reason, black people were not allowed into the Mormon priesthood. In a 1978 revelation from God, however, the prophet Spencer Kimball removed this prohibition. But the question remains, did God curse the Lamanites by giving them dark skin?[17] And did God change his mind?

The comparison between Catholicism and Mormonism pertains to God's revelation. In Catholicism, revelation does not change, but our understanding can be deepened and clarified. In Mormonism, it seems, God can change his mind as with polygamy and in regard to people of color.

While many critics of the Catholic Church, especially Protestants, have tried to discredit her teaching authority, even the few best cases[18] against the Church have reasonable explanations. If this is the best critics can do after 2000 years, it's a miracle.

#5 - Motive

The 5th criterion is motive. That is, do the religious leaders personally benefit in terms of worldly gain, like power, prestige, increased wealth, and sex? Is there an incentive for religious leaders to deceive their followers?

During the first three hundred years of the Catholic Church before Emperor Constantine, there was no motive to become a follower of Christ, except for being drawn by his love and truth. For

---

[17] http://www.equip.org/articles/pinning-down-mormon-doctrine-

http://www.equip.org/articles/pinning-down-mormon-doctrine-part-2-

When Mormons Call, Isaiah Bennet, p.118

[18] For one such case see Pope Honorius, https://www.catholic.com/magazine/print-edition/the-truth-about-pope-honorius

instance:

- Christ allowed only one wife, and there was no divorce or sex outside marriage.
- There was no money to be made; in fact, members were very generous in giving what they had to the poor.
- There was no power. The Church had to operate in secret else suffer martyrdom by Rome. The Roman historian, Tacitus, wrote of what the emperor Nero did to Christians:

> Covered with the skins of beasts, [Christians] were torn by dogs and perished, or were nailed to crosses, or were doomed to the flames and burnt, to serve as nightly illumination when daylight expired.

After Constantine, however, Christianity became the official faith of the empire, then corruption and scandal entered the Church. Today, though, thanks to media and public scrutiny, the Church is becoming morally cleaner and financially poorer; and there is little or no worldly benefit to becoming a Catholic or Church leader right now. We are possibly entering the second holiest period in Church history, next to its first 300 years.

For comparison, while Christianity started in peace and martyrdom for hundreds of years, Islam, under its prophet Muhammad, soon resorted to violent caravan raids and battles which earned them wealth and power.

Also, like Mormonism, Islam allowed polygamy. In fact, in some of Islam's holy writing, for example, the Hadith promises virgins in paradise for shedding one's blood for Allah.[19]

Incidentally, since Islam has no central teaching authority, there is

[19] https://wikiislam.net/wiki/72_Virgins

wide disagreement on their holy texts and how they should be interpreted.

#6 - Love

The sixth criterion, love, is the most essential part of being human. People are willing to die for it – love of children, parents, brothers and sisters; love of boyfriend and girlfriend, husband and wife; love of best friends. Love is what makes us most deeply happy; and when we lose this love, it is traumatic. To put it simply, we are wired for love.

When we consider all creation, from the vast universe to its wonders, such as, the Grand Canyon, does any of it actually impress God? Meaning, did God say to himself, "I am amazed at what I made. I can stare at this forever and be extra happy." I propose the only thing worth being created by God in the entire universe, even in the tiniest amount, is selfless love. And we are wired to recognize this, too. This is why we honor people who have heroically risked life and limb to save others. We even create monuments for those who sacrificed their life.

Consider how small we are in the eyes of the universe and how short our lives are. But Jesus said there is no greater love than to give one's life for a friend. (John 15:13) When a person gives his life, then he has given 100 percent of himself. That 100 percent selfless love is worth all creation.

I cannot think of any other major religion that puts an emphasis on love as does Christianity and Judaism. In fact, the Gospel writer John, states simply in his first letter that, "God is love." (1 John 4:8,16)

Now, if love is so important to the God, then we must confront the existence of evil, hatred, disease, natural disasters, suffering and death, and how they relate to divine love. This was a big issue for me when I did my chaplaincy on a hospital cancer floor where patients ranged in age from 18 to 73. We will consider evil and suffering shortly, but let's continue to look at love in more detail.

As observed earlier, God and other spiritual realities have been kept invisible to us. The reason for this is love.

Free Will

True love must be given freely; it cannot be programmed like a computer robot, nor coerced as in a master-slave relationship, nor conditioned as in Pavlov's dog, and neither is it random. That said, though, how God creates people with free will and still knows how each is going to use it, is a complete mystery.

Words & Invisibility

God's invisibility and his revelation in words are important to our free will. If we could see that God was constantly paying attention to us… if we could look at the great joy of heaven whenever we wanted… if the punishment of hell were always visible… we would have to obey God, and thus lose our freedom to truly love.

To put it another way, God is not terrorizing us to avoid evil with visions of hell, and God is not bribing us to do good with visions of heaven, rather God wants us to choose love freely, even if at great personal cost in this life – because God's type of love is selfless.

Supernatural Signs

As seen in John's Gospel, with divine words God occasionally gives us miraculous signs, i.e., events that cannot be completely explained by science. Even occurrences of supernatural evil, like demonic possession, are signs. We will look at these more in the next criterion about evidence.

Faith

We need faith because spiritual realities are invisible, and God has only given us his words with occasional signs. But Jesus said, "Blessed are those who have not seen and yet believe." (John 20:29b) The Letter to the Hebrews adds, "…faith is the… conviction of things not seen." (Hebrews 11:1)

While faith is a necessary gift from God, this case hopes to show that we need only the tiniest amount of faith to believe, like that of a mustard seed, given the abundance of evidence and how much sense the Catholic faith makes in the context of what we know about life.

#7 - Evidence & Supernatural Signs

There is a great deal of historical and archaeological evidence that traces the Catholic Church back to the Apostles and Christ as well as supports many stories in the Old Testament. This is in contrast to Mormonism, for instance, which has no historical and archaeological evidence for the civilizations and stories in their Book of Mormon, such as the Lamanite people.

In addition to historical and archaeological support, the Catholic Church also has contemporary evidence and miraculous signs. Even instances of supernatural evil are signs.

Try to keep in mind that when we see scientists trying to disprove miraculous events, we should focus on the parts they cannot explain at all, instead of the ones they think they can explain away.

Our Lady of Guadalupe and Juan Diego's Tilma

About 500 years ago, after the Spanish conquered the Aztecs in Mexico, a young Catholic Aztec man, Juan Diego, had a vision of the Lord's mother, Mary. Juan was wearing a native tilma at the time, a cloak made of cactus fiber.

As a sign that his vision was true, Our Lady filled Juan's tilma with Spanish roses and sent him to the bishop. When Juan met the bishop, he uncurled his cloak to let the roses spill to the floor. At that moment, they noticed an image of Our Lady on Juan Diego's tilma.

The nature of this image is such that scientists today cannot determine how to reproduce it from scratch. For instance, no brush strokes can be seen. Further, the fabric itself, made from cactus fiber, should have rotted after 20 years.

Today, almost a half millennium later, Juan Diego's tilma still hangs in the Basilica of Our Lady of Guadalupe in Mexico City.[20]

The Shroud of Turin

The Shroud in Turin, Italy, is the purported burial cloth Jesus was wrapped in at the time of his resurrection. It reveals a *negative* image of a crucified man, complete with nail holes, marks from the Roman whip, wounds from the crown of thorns and many dried blood stains. Like the tilma, scientists do not know how this image was created.[21]

---

[20] Our Lady of Guadalupe, Warren H. Carroll, 2004
https://www.youtube.com/watch?v=2IA5NUHqC88

[21] Shroud: https://www.youtube.com/watch?v=Yzg2ILOxsCY
https://www.shroud.com/

Apparitions

In recent centuries there have been many supposed apparitions of our Lord's mother. One, recently approved by the Church, occurred in Champion, Wisconsin to a young Belgian woman in 1859.[22] Two of the most famous approved apparitions occurred in Lourdes, France and Fatima, Portugal. Both were accompanied by many miracles and cures.

[23]During World War I in Fatima, Portugal, the Mother of Jesus appeared to three young shepherd children, ages 7, 9 and 10, over a six-month period. The last appearance, on October 13, 1917, was public proof that Our Lady was appearing to the children.

Word of the previous apparitions had widely circulated and tens of thousands of people from all around turned out to watch a spectacular miracle. But it had been raining for more than a day, people were drenched, and the roads were muddy. Then, during the apparition, the rain suddenly stopped, clouds parted, and the crowds looked at the sun moving and getting larger without it hurting their eyes. People thought it was going to crash on them, and they became frightened. In a little while, the sun stopped moving and returned to its proper place. Then everyone noticed their clothes were dry, as well as the muddy ground that had pools of water. How everything became instantly dry cannot be explained by mass hallucination.

---

[22] Wisconsin: https://www.catholicnewsagency.com/news/wisconsin-chapel-approved-as-first-us-marian-apparition-site

[23] See Father Andrew Apostoli's book, Fatima for Today, 2012

Miracles toward Canonization of Saints

During the process of researching and canonizing Saints, the Church needs two miracles of the first class for proof where the unexplainable miracle is attributed to the intercessory prayer of the Saint-to-be. In recent years, two such miracles occurred in the Archdiocese of Boston. In one miracle, Deacon Jack Sullivan's spinal cord disorder and severe back pain were inexplicably relieved. His cure was attributed to the intercession of Saint John Henry Cardinal Newman.[24]

In the other miracle, 2-year-old Benedicta McCarthy ate 19 times the lethal dose of Tylenol which caused total kidney failure and deteriorated her liver. Her cure was attributed to the intercession of Edith Stein, also known as Saint Teresa Benedicta of the Cross.[25]

And there have been numerous other miraculous signs throughout the world, such as, physical healings, incorrupt bodies of saints, the stigmata on Padre Pio, blood stained hosts, and weeping statues. However, not all have been sufficiently investigated and approved by the Church.[26]

---

[24] Newman miracle: https://www.youtube.com/watch?v=LP4ozBG5iv4

[25] Stein miracle: https://abcnews.go.com/2020/miracle-benedicta-mccarthy-survived-tylenol-overdose-prayer-sister/story?id=10251732

[26] see Tim Staples, from Catholic Answers, his 7 favorite miracles: https://timstaples.com/2019/the-truth-about-miracles/

#8 - Evil

A true faith from God must be able to explain why there is evil, suffering and death. As discussed earlier, free-will gave us the ability to choose between love and evil. The existence of evil in this world is irrefutable if we only have a little knowledge of history and current events. In fact, when compared to the animal kingdom, it is incomprehensible the evil man can inflict upon other men, women, children, babies, elderly and the disabled -- like holocausts, serial murders, acts of terrorism, mass shootings and other heinous acts.

It was the existence of evil that shocked me into taking my faith seriously more than 20 years ago. At the time, my wife, Marita, was working with a Born-Again Christian man who was challenging her faith. As a result, Marita pressured me about living a more conscientious Catholic life. Anyway, one night I went into the bedroom where she was watching EWTN, a major Catholic cable television network. I crawled in beside her and saw a very disturbing documentary entitled, "The Procedure." But it wasn't the documentary that bothered me most.

In the film, nurse Brenda Pratt Shafer, described what she saw. The doctor used forceps to put the late-term fetus into breach position and delivered the baby feet first until the arms and shoulders were exposed. Then, while the head was still inside the mother, he plunged Metzenbaum scissors into the back of the baby's neck and opened a hole. Nurse Shafer saw the baby's body react to being stabbed. Next, the doctor used a high-powered suction catheter to remove the baby's brains and make the rest of the delivery easier.

When I saw this documentary, I sat up straight! I just couldn't believe it was legal in our country. However, this is not what disturbed me most.

The next morning, I called the offices of my state senator and state representative – two people I knew well, liked, and respected highly. In both instances, their offices told me they fully supported abortion with no restrictions. Then I wondered, how can *good* people support this? At that moment, I stopped following the crowd and doing what everyone else did. I started to think for myself and began researching Scripture and Church teaching.

Evil, we can see, is a mystery of free will. We cannot understand why people choose to do evil, support evil, tolerate evil and fail to recognize evil.

It is also important to notice how evil seeps into culture and takes over, for example, how racism intensified down south and spawned the Ku Klux Klan; how Nazi Germany grew to persecute and exterminate Jews; and how, given ultrasound photos, we came to think abortion is an acceptable medical procedure. Which makes me wonder, what's next? Or rather, who's next?

Though evil is a great mystery, it clearly reflects man's profound freedom to choose between divine love and anti-love.

Satan, Demons & Hell

Interestingly, many Catholics have not given much thought to the strong possibility that Satan and hell exist. Yet the Son of God was crucified to save us from something dire. While this subject will not be easy, we are going to consider it because supernatural evil is one half of the eternal drama.

I don't believe that psychological problems or the Darwinian need to survive fully explains man's evil inspiration, ingenuity and bloodlust. As I write this, it is the 50th anniversary of the Charles Manson murders. Manson and his followers had no connection to the people in that house. Yet, the number of stab wounds on some of the victims was inconceivable. Sharon Tate, who was 8 months pregnant, was stabbed 16 times, 5 of which were each considered fatal.

Many people simply don't believe in the existence of Satan and hell. However, as mentioned earlier, while miracles are signs of God, so diabolic activity indicates the existence of supernatural evil.

William Blatty's popular book, The Exorcist, though fictional, was inspired by a real exorcism decades earlier. The docudrama, "In the Grip of Evil," dramatized the true story and included an interview with a Jesuit who assisted the exorcist as a young priest. In response to skeptics, he calmly said, "All I know is that I was there and I saw it."[27]

Satan and demonic possession are very present in the Gospels. In fact, Jesus himself said, when referring to those who failed to help people with basic needs, like food, clothing and water, that God will say to them, "Depart from me, you cursed, into the eternal fire prepared for the devil and his angels." (Matthew 25:41)

Evil is the result of angels and humans freely choosing to live and act contrary to the love of God. To this day, it boggles my mind that Satan and his angels, who saw and knew God, could still choose to live separated from him. How much easier it is for us, who have not seen God, to walk away from him.

As stated earlier, it became popular in my lifetime to believe hell is empty. But clearly at least Satan and the other fallen angels are there. In fact, possibly one third of the angels rebelled against God. (Revelation 12:3-4)

---

[27] Story that inspired The Exorcist: https://www.washingtonpost.com/wp-srv/style/longterm/movies/features/dcmovies/exorcism1949.htm

For a more contemporary exorcism story see: https://www.ncregister.com/blog/breedail/piccola and interview on https://www.youtube.com/watch?v=YfqRsoBwi58

Since God also loved his angels as he loves us, why should we be surprised that many people likely go to hell, as Jesus warned, "Enter by the narrow gate; for the gate is wide and the way is easy, that leads to destruction, and those who enter by it are many." (Matthew 7:13) That said, however, I am not discounting God's ability to save. Rather, I am affirming our ability to reject God.

Now it hasn't been just Jesus, his disciples and his Church that have warned us about the existence of hell and the reality of judgment, but we have been reminded over time through visions given to saints and apparitions of our Heavenly Mother.

Saints such as Catherine of Siena, Teresa of Avila, and John Bosco have had such visions. Saint Catherine described four ceaseless sufferings of hell: never being able to see God, profound regret, always able to see the ugliness of Satan, and burning in an eternal fire tailored to our sins.[28]

One account that struck me most, though, was during the July apparition of Our Lady to the three children at Fatima when she showed them hell. After the vision, Our Lady said, "You have seen hell where the souls of poor sinners go. To save them God wishes to establish in the world devotion to my immaculate heart. If what I say to you is done, many souls will be saved and there will be peace." Then she taught them a prayer to be said after every decade of the Rosary, "Oh my Jesus, forgive us our sins and save us from the fires of hell. Lead all souls to Heaven, especially those in most need of your mercy."[29] If our Holy Mother showed *children* hell, then shouldn't we pay attention?

I was also surprised by our Lord's vision to Saint Faustina. She received revelations from Jesus in Poland prior to World War II. As

---

[28] The Fulfillment of All Desire, 2006, Ralph Martin, p.52-54

[29] Fatima for Today, p.60, 66

a result of these private revelations, the Church celebrates the Sunday after Easter as Divine Mercy Sunday. In fact, Jesus' mercy is the central theme of these revelations. But she, too, was given a vision of hell. Then at the end of this vision she wrote, "I am writing this at the command of God, so that no soul may find an excuse by saying there is no hell, or that nobody has ever been there and so no one can say what it is like."[30]

The existence of hell is a troublesome and even scary reality to consider, because it is horrible in every respect and eternal. But I see three positive aspects to it.

First, God allows evil so he can bring greater love out of it. Remember this verse from the Easter Vigil, "O happy fault, O necessary sin of Adam, which gained for us, so great a Redeemer!" – Meaning, without original sin, there would be no Jesus. Saint Paul, taught, "…where sin increased, grace abounded all the more…" (Romans 5:20) Thus in a sense, evil makes saints.

Second, the intense suffering of this world, the gruesome reality of Christ's sacrifice on the cross, centuries of martyrs, and many other evils, suggest how dramatically and eternally significant our faith lives are. If life were not about salvation, why else would God allow such suffering?

Third, hell is very motivating, because I care about my eternal life, the lives of those I love, and of those I don't know. As children of God, each of us has a divine mission to fulfill.

Saint Paul wrote, "Put on the whole armor of God, that you may be able to stand against the wiles of the devil. For we are not contending against flesh and blood, but against the principalities, against the powers, against the world rulers of this present darkness, [and] against the spiritual hosts of wickedness in heavenly places..."

[30] Diary of Saint Maria Faustina Kowalska, Marian Press, #741

(Ephesians 6:11-12)

Saint Peter warned, "Be sober, be watchful. Your adversary the devil prowls around like a roaring lion, seeking someone to devour." (1 Peter 5:8)

Satanism

Satanism, the religion of Satan, works. Thus, the Church warns us against tapping into supernatural forces outside of Jesus Christ and the Church, such as, sorcery, horoscopes, mediums, conjuring up the dead, Ouija boards, etc. (CCC 2115-17) It was reported in 2004 that Pope John Paul II told every diocese they should have an assigned exorcist. (Washington Post, May 20, 2016)

Satan as an Angel of Light

Saint Paul made an interesting observation about the devil when he wrote, "…even Satan disguises himself as an angel of light. So, it is not strange if his servants also disguise themselves as servants of righteousness." (2 Corinthians 11:14-15) I think this happened when priests wearing Roman collars were trusted by parents and molested their children.

Interestingly, the founders of Islam and Mormonism each claimed to receive their revelation from an angel. Assuming Mohammed and Joseph Smith were sincere, and it was not a hoax, Satan might be an explanation to divert people away from Christianity.

Likewise, some people sincerely believe they saw aliens and UFOs. If there were no natural explanations, then it's possible they, too, were deceived by Satan.

When there are purported apparitions of Our Lady, or miraculous events, the Church investigates and waits a long time before approving them – because she knows Satan can be disguising himself as an angel of light.

In the next two sections, let's see why God, who is love, allows suffering, and how suffering and death lead to glory.

#9 - Suffering & Love

My friend became an atheist because terrible suffering exists. He experienced a profound loss when his dad, a city cab driver, was murdered while on the job. Importantly, therefore, horrible suffering must be reconcilable with "God who is love." (1 John 4: 8, 16)

Of course, we know suffering is at the heart of Christianity, because the beloved Son of God was crucified. But how does it relate to love?

A year before ordination, I was assigned to part-time chaplaincy on a cancer floor at a major Boston hospital. For 10 weeks, three nights a week, I went to the hospital after work to visit patients ranging in age from 18 to 73. I met people at all stages of the process, from initial discovery until death. In that short period of time, I saw a lot of suffering, some anger and fear.

I remember walking into one room where a daughter and son, in their late teens, stood near the wall, motionless and without expression. Their mother was curled up in bed, in a fetal position. Her head was bald, and she was absorbed in discomfort. Two weeks earlier, she did not know she was sick.

When chaplaincy was over, I went on a scheduled retreat. I had one agenda item for God. Since God is love, I needed to know how suffering was related to divine love. I believe the Lord gave me some simple insights.

First, let me say what heavenly love is not. It is not loving the stuff of this world, as Jesus said, "Do not lay up for yourselves treasure on earth… but lay up for yourselves treasure in heaven." "For where your treasure is, there will your heart be also." (Matthew 6:19-21)

Second, divine love is not simply loving those who love us back. Jesus said, "If you love those who love you, what credit is that to you? Even sinners love those who love them" (Luke 6:32) "and give good gifts to their children." (Matthew 7:11)

Essentially, divine love is loving like God. It is a love that is heroic, unsung heroic, faithful, generous and merciful.

It is giving abundantly to those who are suffering with no prospect of being paid back, thanked or appreciated. At its peak, this generous love is always forgiving and merciful. That is, we are called to keep giving even to those who are ungrateful… we are called to keep doing good even to those who harm us… (Luke 6:35) and we are called to remain faithful and committed… because this is how God loves us.

When we are in a plight and life seems drastically unfair, and God is not helping as we want, and he seems distant and uncaring, we might even have to forgive God and remain faithful to him... because this is how God loves us.

We must understand this. We were made in the image and likeness of God. We were baptized children of God, brothers and sisters of Jesus, and heirs to the Kingdom. Therefore, to share in God's divinity forever, we are called to love like God, whether we feel like it or not.

When an earthquake or tsunami devastates a desperately poor country, it's like God shouting to the first world, "Remember to care for me in the poor, ill and hopeless," as Jesus taught, "Truly, I say to you, as you did it to one of the least of these my brothers [and sisters], you did it to me." (Matthew 25:40)

Not long ago, during a homily, the pastor brought a challenging statistic to our attention. You know how the media loves to vilify the wealthiest 1% in our country, like the millionaires and billionaires? The fact is we are among the wealthiest 1% of the world. I think this fact should cause us to consider the beam in our own eye. That is, as a percentage of our wealth, to what extent are we helping the world's poor?

While we cannot understand why particular tragedies occur, we can know in general why God allows people to suffer. As Christ, they offer us salvation and the opportunity to love like God. As we will see in the next section, those who suffer can also glorify God and be his witnesses on earth.

#10 - Death & Glory

On the cancer floor, I visited a third-year college student. He discovered his illness one day when he tried to go out for a run, but quickly became unusually tired. After a couple of weeks of this, he went to the doctors. When I met him, he was receiving the fourth of six chemo treatments for lymphoma.

I told him about a woman patient I met who, after fighting cancer for 4 years, was in hospice dying. I was amazed at her faith and serenity even though she was leaving behind a child in middle school. Astonishingly, the young man said, his mother fought cancer for 4 years and died when he was twelve, and his brothers were even younger.

Then he said, "My father is a protestant minister and at his church, people would ask my mother, 'Why? Why did God do this to you?' She would always answer, 'Why not me? If God chooses to use my suffering for his glory… why not me?'"

When he said this, I didn't immediately get the connection between his mother's suffering and God's glory. In time, though, it became clear.

Like Job, when God seems to take everything away from us, and we still remain faithful to him, then we are glorifying God, because we are loving him the way he loves us. This is a type of martyrdom or witness. Throughout Christian history some were given a choice, "Deny Christ and you will not suffer." These martyrs chose to suffer rather than abandon Jesus. For other martyrs, like the young man's mother above, Job, and Rosie's parents (Laura + Charlie), they were afflicted with suffering first. Then their choice was to remain faithful to God or leave him. All martyrs share in our Lord's Passion. In their affliction, they complete Christ's suffering (Colossians 1:24) for the salvation of souls.

When we strive to live lives that glorify God, death becomes something not to be feared, but the moment of victory. It becomes the eternal goal line; the end zone where we enter Heaven, into complete union with the Holy Trinity and all the Saints and Angels – a union full of everlasting peace, joy and love in God's family.

Through our faithful love, strengthened by God, we defeat the power of darkness as it is written in the last book of the Bible, "They conquered [Satan] by the blood of the Lamb and by the word of their testimony; love for [this] life did not deter them from death." (Revelation 12:11)

#11 – A Sixth Sense for Knowing God

Sensory feelings are important. When my son was about two years old, the burner on the gas stove was lit. Before I could react, he stretched out his little hand toward the flame saying, "Blue." After he felt the pain of fire, he never did it again.

In a similar way, when relating to people, we experience emotions. As the pain in my son's hand told him to stop touching the flame, emotions (positive and negative) alert us about other people and about what's going on inside ourselves.

That said, our emotions, like feelings, are not always correct. For instance, I have an unreasonable fear of heights. I remember trying to hike the Grand Canyon with my sons. But between their horse-playing, the narrow paths, and sharp turns where you can't see what's coming around the corner, I couldn't do it. Thinking rationally, though, my sons and I have never fallen off a sidewalk or driveway, so my feelings were not in sync with reality.

It is a common tendency for people to make decisions based on emotion. Advertisers, politicians, entertainers, and many others purposely appeal to our emotions like anger, fear, desire, exhilaration, love and a sense of belonging.

In this book, I have tried to get us to think through our feelings because we cannot allow our emotions to control us, rather we must manage them. We cannot make life altering decisions simply based on feelings.

That said, however, it is important for us to pay attention to our emotions. And some of these come from God.

The Lord speaks to us constantly through creation, events in our lives, other people, and most directly and clearly through Sacred Scripture and Church teaching. As we listen to God, we will experience feelings like consolation, peace, joy, guilt, sorrow, forgiveness, tender love and encouragement. God loves us as our perfect Father and he wants us to feel his warmth, support and inspiration.

When I was in college there was a perfect storm in my life and I started asking big questions like, "Why am I here?" and "What is the purpose of my life?" Then for the first time I picked up the family Bible. I remember being moved by special feelings while reading the Beatitudes -- "Blessed are the poor in spirit… Blessed are those who mourn… Blessed are the meek…" (Matthew chapter 5) A strong feeling struck me and I thought, God cares about most people… you know, the ones few notice, while the world cares about the rich and famous. That is, God sees things upside-down compared to how the world sees things.

These special feelings are a sixth sense for knowing God, as real as our other five senses. I hate to be quaint on this important point, but it's often like ET's heart glowing. Tangible experiences of God represent the eleventh reason why I believe.

In Luke's Gospel (24:32), two of Jesus' disciples had this special feeling. They said to each other, "Did not our hearts burn as we spoke to Jesus along the road and he explained the scriptures to us?"

To reiterate, however, we must be careful about feelings. For instance, the Mormons try to influence people through their emotions. They call it a "fire in one's bosom." But this is an example of why feelings must be subordinate to evidence and reason. That is, there are so many other aspects of their faith that don't add up, such as no historical and archaeological evidence for their holy book's history; God changing his mind on polygamy and whether dark people can become priests; and the motive of enticing men by allowing many wives. We cannot simply follow our feelings and desires.

#12 - Reason

Throughout this book, I have used evidence and reason to demonstrate that the Catholic faith is most likely the one true faith given to us by God. All other options, from atheism and secularism to various ancient and modern beliefs, fall short on one or more significant criteria as illustrated in a few examples.

First, we looked at evidence for God: how even time started with the Big Bang; the impossible mathematical probability that one moment has followed the next until now; and how Darwinism cannot explain our appreciation for beauty, unless it's a mistake. Atheists, in contrast, believe one day scientists will be able to explain all this. Given the enormous expanse of the universe, however, that's a huge leap of faith for tiny earthlings with 3-pound brains.

As with the existence of God, what really tilts things toward Catholicism is more evidence. The Catholic Church completely affirms the history of the Jews from creation to Jesus as presented in the Old Testament. Moreover, for 2,000 years, the Church has observed miracles, apparitions, and diabolic activity to this current day – occurrences that cannot be adequately explained by science.

Not only that, all this evidence ties together and makes sense, like pieces in a puzzle. For instance:

- The only reason for God creating human beings, tiny and short-lived, is that they may choose to love self-sacrificially like Jesus, because selflessly giving 100%, is still a 100%, no matter the size.
- God gives us his words and signs, while keeping spiritual realities invisible, so we may freely choose between divine love or evil, i.e., living for eternal life or living for this life.
- It is possible for God, that all words are true in Sacred Scripture and official Church teaching on faith and morals, when properly

understood. In fact, it makes no sense that the beloved Son of God and Word Made Flesh would suffer on a cross only to leave us confused about his words. To the contrary, in Church teaching, all words of the Bible are arranged like musical notes in a symphonic score or stars in the night sky.

- Finally, as in the first centuries of Christianity, today there is no worldly benefit and motive to being a Catholic or Church leader. In fact, in this modern age coupled with horrific Church scandals and controversial moral teaching, it might bring ridicule and persecution.

So, the Catholic Church stands up well when we consider evidence and the evaluative criteria just used. The Church does well because she was historically founded by Christ and remains protected, inspired and guided by the Holy Spirit. What other institution has endured for two thousand years with so many enemies? What other institution has inspired so many saints, like Saint Mother Teresa of Calcutta and Saint Francis of Assisi, and other Catholics who selflessly care for those in need? We have so much to be grateful for and so much treasure at our fingertips. This is actually a great time and place to be a Catholic, because Christ and his Church need us.

At this point, now, given that Catholicism is most likely the true faith given to us by God, let's address some problems and challenges.

Only a Little Faith Is Needed

I have referred to science, math, history, etc., to help us see the truth of our faith. I have also presented some miracles and signs that cannot be explained by science. Now we are going to look at four examples where what we believe cannot be demonstrated by material analysis.

First Parents

First, geneticist Francis Collins, author of The Language of God, believes there were about 10,000 first parents. However, the Church teaches everyone descends from one set of first parents, Adam and Eve. This is a matter of faith we must accept even though science does not fully support it, yet.

The beauty of the Church position is we are all blood relatives, truly one human family. Contrast this to the idea of descending from many sets of first parents, and we might be tempted to think one race is more human or highly evolved than another. Looking back at slavery and Nazism, we see how this can end.

Resurrection

Second, the Church teaches Jesus rose from the dead a couple of days after he died on the cross, which cannot be proven today aside for the Shroud of Turin and ancient witness accounts. Jesus definitely died – the crucifixion was brutal, and a Roman soldier thrust a spear into his side to make sure he was dead before taking him down. The apostles, who went into hiding out of fear, saw the resurrection as proof Jesus is who he said he was – the Son of God with power over death. (cf. John 10:18) What else explains their later courageousness to spread the faith and suffer martyrdom?

Thomas, however, did not initially see the risen Jesus when his fellow apostles did. He would not believe their word until he touched Christ's wounds himself. The risen Jesus confronted Thomas on this and said, "Blessed are they who have not seen, yet believe." (John 20:29)

Eucharist

Third, the Church teaches us that the bread and wine at Mass become, in reality, the body, blood, soul and divinity of Jesus Christ, the Son of God. The Church bases this on the traditional understanding going back to the apostles and on what Jesus said, especially as recorded in the Gospel of John (6:26-69) and the Last Supper narratives.

Jesus said to a multitude who followed him, "Do not labor for the food which perishes, but for the food which endures to eternal life… I am the bread of life…"

At this, the people murmured, and Jesus responded, "Do not murmur among yourselves. I am the living bread which came down from heaven; if anyone eats this bread, he will live forever; and the bread which I shall give for the life of the world is my flesh."

The Jews and his disciples disputed among themselves, exclaiming, "This is a hard saying; who can listen to it? How can this man give us his flesh to eat?"

So, Jesus insisted, "Truly, truly, I say to you, unless you eat the flesh of the Son of man and drink his blood, you have no life in you; he who eats my flesh and drinks my blood has eternal life, and I will raise him up at the last day. For my flesh is food indeed, and my blood is drink indeed. He who eats my flesh and drinks my blood abides in me, and I in him."

After this many of his disciples drew back and no longer went about with him. Then Jesus asked the twelve [apostles], "Do you wish to go away, too?"

Violence in the Bible

Finally, in the 2nd criterion, The Words of God, I listed some reasons and Church teaching for believing that all words in the Bible are true when properly understood. But a common criticism of our faith today centers around violent stories in the Old Testament and how these cannot be reconciled with a God who is love. Interestingly, even some early Church fathers wrestled with these problems.

When reading these accounts, we must first distinguish, are these simply the evil actions of people, or is it something God did or commanded. Just because people did it in the Bible, doesn't mean it was approved by God.

We must understand that God's revelation to mankind occurred progressively in stages. Jesus was not born in the beginning, but thousands of years later. In the first stage, when we study ancient history, we see how evil people can be when they do not have the words of God, such as, human and child sacrifice.

From the start, though, God was preparing a chosen people. In the time of Moses, he gave his people the Ten Commandments, and later many other laws. This was to make them better and more holy. However, like today, some neglected and disobeyed God. In fact, their hearts were so hardened, Moses even loosened some laws, such as on divorce. (Matthew 19:3-9)

Following Moses, came the prophets with even more instructions about how people should love God and neighbor. But many still didn't listen and the laws were difficult to live up to.

In the last stage, where we are today, God sent his only beloved son, the divine word made flesh. Jesus referred to the Old Testament many times in his teaching. And it's through Jesus that the entire Bible makes sense.

However, Jesus did not just leave us his words, because from the time of Moses, words themselves were not enough. Rather, Jesus established a single permanent hierarchical Church to guide and nourish his people. Moreover, he told his disciples to wait until they receive the Holy Spirit, because it is through the Sacraments that we become temples of the Holy Spirit and are given the divine gifts necessary to love like God. And it is through the protection, inspiration, and power of the Holy Spirit, that the Church can nourish us with her sacraments and guide us with official instruction.

So, during the Old Testament, God was gradually struggling to prepare a holy people despite their resistance. Remember, how they rebelled against Moses and God soon after escaping Egypt. Therefore, the sinful actions tolerated by God then, does not mean they were endorsed by God. This is similar to parents raising teenagers and young adults. Like the father of the prodigal son, we might have to tolerate some bad choices and pray our children get back on track.

Clearly, with New Testament hindsight, people in the Old Testament committed many immoral acts, and some of these were tolerated by God as he tried to progressively make his people holy. However, through these stories we learned that people cannot love like God on their own, or even with just his words. Rather, people need Christ's sacrifice, his Church and the indwelling action of his Holy Spirit.

Violent Acts Committed or Commanded by God

Some faithful believe we should treat God's violent acts as allegorical, suggesting they didn't really happen, but were written to dramatically teach spiritual lessons. This is akin to saying that Jesus' warnings about damnation were to increase our concern but were otherwise empty threats.

My position is, if the biblical text reads like history, then it's best to believe it, even if the text is initially difficult to accept. Therefore, I believe God committed and commanded certain violent acts as written. For instance, I believe Jesus meant what he said when he warned,

> "As were the days of Noah, so will be the coming of the Son of man. For as in those days before the flood they were eating and drinking, marrying and giving in marriage, until the day when Noah entered the ark. They did not know until the flood came and swept them all away. So, will be the coming of the Son of man. Then two men will be in the field; one is taken and one is left. Two women will be grinding at the mill; one is taken and one is left. Watch therefore, for you do not know on what day your Lord is coming." (Matthew 24:37-42)

When God committed or commanded certain violent acts, we have to trust his judgment. We don't know to what extent the people deserved it; or possibly for some, this was their punishment before entering heaven; or maybe younger ones perished before they could sin. I don't know. But I am sure of this – these violent historical acts of God dramatically underscore how crucial it is to take our spiritual lives seriously and practice the faith. Noah, who was a righteous man and walked with God, brought his family into his saving ship. And so it is today, where the Church is like Noah's ship.

Possible for God

Our faith requires us to trust and believe certain things. But isn't all this possible for God? One pair of first parents truly making all humanity one family; the resurrection of Jesus from the dead, proof of his divinity and power over death; the transformation of bread and wine into the body and blood of Christ while retaining the appearance of bread and wine, an intimate way to take Jesus into our bodies; and the truthfulness of all God's words. Can we humble ourselves enough to see this is possible for God?

Some Protestants criticize the Catholic Church for not being Scriptural. But the real problem is the Catholic Church believes in Scripture too much, for which I am grateful.

After Jesus asked, "Do you wish to go away, too?" Peter replied, "Lord, to whom shall we go? You have the words of eternal life… you are the Holy One of God."

If we do not believe and follow Jesus, who will we follow? Has God spoken to any of us from a burning bush? Are any of us God-made-man like Jesus? Where but in the Church, does all we know about life and reality fit so well together?

The Jews found the teaching of Jesus that they must consume his body and blood, revolting and impossible to accept. They weren't even allowed to consume animal blood, never mind human blood. Despite his numerous miracles and authoritative teaching, many walked away from Jesus.

While we might not be bothered by Jesus' words concerning his body and blood, there are some things about the Church that trouble us in today's culture.

Addressing the Problems

Sex

In the past 50 years the Church has found herself on the wrong side of some very popular cultural issues. So, I would be negligent if I did not discuss a particularly strong obstacle to our faith. It is the 800-pound gorilla that Catholics largely overlook – the Church's teaching on sexual relations. This includes, for instance, prohibitions against pornography, masturbation, homosexual actions, sex outside of marriage, adultery, abortion, in-vitro fertilization and artificial contraception.

For a moment let us drop preconceived notions that this teaching erroneously comes from a group of white celibate men who hate sex and are out of touch with modern times. To the contrary, the Church actually holds the sexual act in the highest esteem. In the eyes of God and the Church, sex is holy. Let me say this again – sexual union is a sacred act.

When we think about it, it's obvious. We were made in the image and likeness of God (Genesis 1:27)… our body is a temple of the Holy Spirit within (1 Corinthians 6:19)… and during the sexual act when circumstances are right, a child is conceived. In that moment, the mother, father and God create a child with a mind, body and soul, who will live forever.

As I stated earlier, my wife challenged me to take my faith more seriously and I began to study Scripture and Church teaching using the Bible and Catechism. Then I discovered the instruction on artificial contraception. I shared this with my wife. We did some more investigation and about a year later our youngest was born. Joe has brought a lot of joy to our house and his older brothers love him.

During my study, the Scripture verse that affected me most is where the prophet Malachi (2:15) said the Lord wants "Godly offspring" from marriage. That is, he wants holy children who grow to love God and neighbor more than oneself.

This makes perfect sense. God, whose very nature is a loving family, wants us to generously conceive and raise holy children who will be united with him forever. God wants a HUGE LOVING FAMILY – and he asks us to help him create it.

Many Catholics find it difficult to accept the teaching authority of the Church, especially when it comes to their "bedroom." But is sex so powerful that we cannot live without it for a period of time and make this sacrifice for God? Is there anything we will not give, if God asks?

When we see all Scripture and Church teaching tie together with what we profoundly know about life and reality, we have no choice, but in all conscience, to embrace God's revelation. Where else can we go? (cf. John 6:68)

While commanding my boys when they were very young, I used to look down at them and ask, "Who's the boss?" And they would look straight up and flippantly respond with a smile, "We are."

Well, parents are the boss. But even as grownups, we are still God's children and he is our Father. So, "Who is our boss?" One thing is certain, I am not the master of the universe.

We are tempted to think, even with small minds, that we know more than God, and he and his words must be wrong because they conflict with what we want. However, we must be patient and trust God to help us understand, for the teaching of the Church is holy. When we fully accept what God is saying, we become much happier, joyful and peaceful.

Sin

Sin is an action or inaction contrary to God's love that harms us or others. Since whatever we do to ourselves and others, we do to Jesus (Matthew 25), we can conclude that when we sin, we in a real sense hurt Jesus. No matter how personal, private and mutually consenting that sin is, we undermine holiness and contribute to the power of evil in the world. Jesus taught, "Not everyone who says to me, 'Lord, Lord,' shall enter the kingdom of heaven, but he who does the will of my Father who is in heaven." (Matthew 7:21)

Saint Paul warned, "the works of the flesh are plain: fornication, impurity, licentiousness, idolatry, sorcery, enmity, strife, jealousy, anger, selfishness, dissension, party spirit, envy, drunkenness, carousing, and the like. I warn you, as I warned you before, that those who do such things shall not inherit the kingdom of God." (Galatians 5:19-21) And Jesus used a similar list when describing what defiles a man. (Mark 7:20-23)

One of greatest gifts we have in the Church is the ability to go to confession for the Sacrament of Reconciliation and have Jesus say to us, through his priest, "Your sins are forgiven." On the evening of his resurrection, Jesus entered the room where the disciples were hiding and said, "Peace be with you. As the Father has sent me, I send you." Then he "breathed on them" and said, "Receive the Holy Spirit. If you forgive the sins of any, they are forgiven; if you retain the sins of any, they are retained." (cf. John 20:18-23)

Many Protestants and even Catholics disagree with the Church as to what constitutes sin, and believe they can receive God's forgiveness without a priest. But it is God, through Jesus and his Church, who defines what love and sin are, including deadly or mortal sins (CCC 1861). God also gives us the Sacrament of Reconciliation (CCC 1440) for divine forgiveness. Furthermore, no matter how good, bad, understanding or knowledgeable the priest is himself, the sacraments still work.

We can receive the Sacrament of Reconciliation frequently, especially when we're struggling against sinful inclinations. Through God's forgiveness our souls are healed, and we are given renewed strength.

Interestingly, all sin seems to begin with temptation followed by disobedience, just like the original sin of Adam and Eve. As we persist in sin, it may become hard-wired as in a vice you don't want to give up or an addiction. But remember, it first began with disobedience.

After a while, if we continue to sin, our conscience weakens, and we begin to rationalize it. Then we may start defending and promoting this disobedience even to our own children. In fact, disobedience may have been passed down to us.

We must understand that we cannot expect to enter heaven and complete union with God – heart, mind and soul – while remaining defiant. God will not accept us on our own terms. Rather, we must stand before God as humble docile children in need of forgiveness.

God never tires of healing and strengthening us through his Sacraments, such as, Confession. And we need his grace to be holy.

Scandal

From the time of Judas, the Church has always had, and always will have, sinners who commit major scandals – sexual, financial, etc. Jesus warned about this. He foresaw that the Church would have wolves in sheep's clothing (cf. Matthew 7:15) and that weeds would grow with the wheat until the end of time when the weeds would be gathered and burned. (cf. Matthew 13:24-30) And about Judas, he said it would be better for him if he had never been born. (cf.

Matthew 26:24) In the end, there is ultimate justice. No one is going to get away with anything.

Doubts & Disbelief

How can a man and woman have a deep, intimate, personal, and trusting relationship, as in marriage, if the other's words cannot be fully believed? Every falsehood is a deformity in a relationship where the two are unable to fully connect as one.

And, so it is with all our doubts and disbeliefs in the words of God – that is, our misgivings about Sacred Scripture and Church teaching. Every doubt weakens our relationship with God and dampens our enthusiasm and resolve. When allowed to fester, doubt and disbelief can become opposition that affects the faith of our loved ones, friends and acquaintances.

To help counter doubts and opposition, I have shared with you why I am convinced that it takes only the tiniest amount of faith to be wholeheartedly Catholic, while all other options require enormous leaps of faith that defy evidence and reason. Thus, it makes no sense to follow one's imagination about who God is, because he is not visibly speaking to any of us individually in ways that contradict Sacred Scripture and Church teaching.

Likewise, God has not given any of us the authority to reject or be passive aggressive about any of the Church's teaching. Moreover, it makes no sense to hedge our bets by trying to have it our way and God's way. No one enters heaven without being ready for complete union with God.

Jesus said, "I am… the truth…" (John 14:6) and "the truth will make you free." (John 8:32b) The Church established by Christ offers us the fullness of truth. In the words of Saint Peter, "Where else can we go?"

Yes, people can be "good" in the eyes of society while disagreeing with the Church and not going to Mass. But God is calling us to be much greater than "good." He wants us to be perfectly holy. (Matthew 5:48) He wants us to be divine. In fact, only saints and angels are in heaven.

Can We Trust God?

Believing God's words can be pretty easy when life is basically going well. There are times, though, when God's words seem completely unreasonable. Maybe circumstances get extra difficult and we need a way out; or we're facing a huge moral challenge; or God is inspiring us to do something we don't feel prepared for. This is when we have to move from belief to trust – **trust** in God's love, guidance, support and ultimate happiness.

A priest told this story. His niece married a Lutheran man and became pregnant. But the baby had a medical condition where the doctors knew he would die soon after delivery. Of course, the doctors offered his niece a quick way out.

She called her uncle. Interestingly, the priest did not tell her what to do, but trusted she would make the right decision.

The time for delivery came and some pro-life nurses were there to offer support. Everyone prayed. Then the baby was born just as the doctors expected. For the next hour or so, the baby was passed from person to person, where they hugged and kissed the baby, until he died. The niece's husband was so moved by this experience, he became a Catholic.

Sometimes we must trust God despite what seems to make more sense, then look for his tender mercies.

The Role of Women in the Church

A big issue for many is that women cannot be ordained priests. As the Church says we need water for baptism, and bread and wine for the Eucharist, so she says we need men for the sacrament of ordination to priesthood – because, for instance, priests represent Christ on earth; Jesus was a man; his Apostles were men; and the Church has only ever ordained men. Out of all the issues, this is the Church position I accept mostly on faith.

In a Fall 2014 interview on 60 Minutes,[31] Nora O'Donnell challenged Cardinal Sean O'Malley when she asserted women have very little power in the Church and are second-class citizens. Then she called it unfair and immoral. Let's consider 60 Minutes' criticisms centered on fairness and power.

First, we must observe that life, from a human perspective, is extremely unfair. For instance, we didn't get to pick the time, place and circumstances of our birth. Throughout history and around the world, most people were born into difficult situations or worse. This unfairness is so pervasive and out of people's control, that we have to conclude it's by God's design as he knew from the moment before creation how it would all play out. Therefore, something that seems unfair to us can still be the will of God.

Second, as for women having little power, Cardinal Sean said the Church is about service, not power. I suspect only the tiniest fraction of viewers understood Cardinal Sean's words. But he was spot on.

In the Bible, I cannot recall a single instance where Jesus praised worldly power as something to be sought. Yet, I remember his

---

[31] https://www.cbsnews.com/news/cardinal-sean-omalley-works-with-pope-francis-to-reform-catholic-church/

mother's words. Her response to the angel's request was,

> "I am the **handmaid** of the Lord, let it be done to me according to your word." (Luke 1:38)

Then, after conceiving Jesus in her womb, Mary went in haste to visit her cousin Elizabeth. In response to her greeting, Mary proclaimed,

> "My soul magnifies the Lord and my spirit rejoices in God my savior. For he has looked with favor on his **lowly servant**. From this day, all generations will call me blessed for the Mighty God has done great things for me." (Luke 1:46-49)

We should carefully note that this lowly handmaid mother of Jesus, a poor woman and wife who raised Jesus on the other side of the tracks in Nazareth, is the highest-ranking creature in heaven, for all eternity, even higher than the angels. Her titles include Queen of Heaven and Mother of God.

The highest position in heaven was given to a lowly servant woman. Not a pope, bishop or priest; not a military general or business tycoon. This exemplifies the words of Jesus when he said, "Blessed are the poor and meek." (cf. Luke 6:20 and Matthew 5:1-12)

In addition to our Holy Mother, notice what other women in the Church have accomplished throughout the centuries when women had little or no power in society unless they were a queen. They became Saints, Doctors of the Church, and founders of vast religious orders and organizations.

In our time, look at what Saint Mother Teresa accomplished as well as Mother Angelica. The Missionaries of Charity have thousands of religious sisters and brothers caring for the poorest of the poor all around the world. Mother Angelica founded EWTN, the largest religious media network in the world. These women, blessed by God, created vast ministries out of nothing.[32]

Therefore, we cannot criticize the Church based on fairness and power, as this seems to place us against God. We have to trust that God knows what he is doing.

Now we might ask does God have a practical reason for a male-only priesthood? I can only speculate that men, who have usually been more powerful, are therefore more difficult to save. And maybe a male priesthood will have more success getting through to men.

Given this understanding, if I had daughters, I would raise them to compete and succeed, but I would also raise them to be loving and discerning, and to trust God and his Church.

---

[32] Amazon Prime has movies and documentaries about the life of Saint Mother Teresa. Also, see Raymond Arroyo's 2007 book, Mother Angelica: The Remarkable Story. This is a very interesting and fun read. One of my favorite books.

Salvation

Eternal Salvation

We must keep in mind that God our Father loves all of us more than we can imagine. He wants everyone to be saved (1 Tim 2:4) and desires that no one will perish (2 Pet 3:9). The eternally dramatic question is, however, "Will we respond to his love, with love?"

While this can be a terrifying situation to ponder, the reality is, according to Church teaching, there are ultimately only two eternal destinations – heaven or hell. (CCC 1022) And it does us no good to ignore or deny this fact. At the same time, though, God has made his loving mercy easily available.

The reason I wrote this book is out of concern for people's salvation because so many are neglecting and forgetting Jesus. My hope is loved ones will encourage each other so they may be prepared when it is time to stand before God, the father of Jesus crucified.

We live in an era where almost everyone presumes they will go to heaven, whether or not they went to church, and whether or not they got to know Jesus. People compare themselves to those who are horribly evil and conclude they must be good enough. "After all, God can't send everyone to hell." But they never paid attention to Jesus' actual words and thus never took them to heart. In a parable Jesus said, "Many will come to the door and say, 'Lord let us in.' But I will say, 'I do not know you.'" (cf. Luke 13:23-28, Matthew 25:1-13) Which is absurd since Jesus is God and knows everything. Rather, he's really saying, we do not know him. That is, Jesus is not a beloved member of our family.

Practicing Catholics, through revelation, know that the one God is an intimate and complete union of three eternal persons – Father, Son and Holy Spirit. That is God, in his very nature, is a divine loving family and Holy Trinity. Thus, heaven is for children of God who want to be in intimate communion with the Holy Trinity.

Jesus said, "He who sees me, sees [God the] Father." (cf. John 12:45) "The Father and I are one." (cf. John 10:30) "Father, as I am in you and you are in me, may they be one in us." (cf. John 17:21) "He who eats my flesh and drinks my blood abides in me, and I in him." (John 6:56)

The closest analogy we have in this life to that divine communion is when a husband and wife come together, and through their permanent loving union, create a child with God who will live forever.

But how can we expect intimate communion with God having not trusted his words and without getting to know each other over time? Like, what man and woman, when they first meet, immediately get married and start a family?

Or suppose I had 10 children. As soon as they were old enough nine moved far away and never called or visited me. I never even met their children. But one child stayed with me and cared for me in my old age. How should I divide my modest estate? How is God going to share his inheritance with us?

Professor Martin noted that Saint Catherine of Siena is one of several saints who had a vision of hell. She said, God doesn't so much send people to hell, but each soul "rushes" to where they want to be. Martin concluded, "In a very real way each person chooses their own destiny over the course of their own lifetime and, at the moment of death, embraces what has truly become their choice."[33]

[33] The Fulfillment of All Desire, 2006, Ralph Martin, p.59

Mercy

As I stated in the beginning, we live in a time when it is truly easy to receive God's mercy. All we have to do is turn away from sin; attend Sunday Mass and on holy days of obligation; take God's words to heart daily; and go to confession periodically. This is just an hour on the weekend, a few minutes of prayer each day, a periodic trip to confession, and a couple of extra Masses each year on holy days. That's all it takes, so we may be prepared to stand before God.

But do we care enough for God to give up sin and practice the faith Jesus gave us?

Hope

No one is too difficult for God to save, regardless of what we've done, and no matter how stuck we are in sin. Even those we love who have gone before us, and those stuck in the ways of the world today, can be saved by God, if we will only pray for them. Only God can judge and only God knows how much each person is responsible. Saint James made it clear when he wrote that "mercy triumphs over judgement." (James 2:13b) That said, we must not presume upon God's mercy, but rather do our part to remain faithful and pray for loved ones.

With this in mind, we should always have hope in God's desire and power to save, and never despair. I cannot remember any of the Apostles getting depressed. Rather, no matter the difficulty, they were filled with the joy of the Holy Spirit and Good News. And we must be, too.

Worldly Salvation

The emphasis in this book has been on ensuring our eternal salvation so we may live in union with God in heaven. However, it's important to recognize what we will lose during this lifetime on earth to the extent we and the world neglect and forget Jesus.

When we walk away from Jesus, and accept sin in our lives, we should expect natural consequences, such as, broken relationships, stress, depression, crime and so forth. On the other hand, if we take our Lord's words to heart and practice our faith, we should anticipate much greater peace and joy. This pertains to the world, too.

Saving the World

When we look at God's saving acts in the Old Testament, it had mostly a worldly focus, such as, escape from Egyptian bondage and protection from other enemy kingdoms. However, when the Jews forgot God's words and ignored the prophets, then they were brutally conquered by foreign nations – the Assyrians about 700 BC, Babylonians near 600 BC and finally when the Romans reconquered Jerusalem and destroyed its temple in 70 AD, about 40 years after the crucifixion.

In the New Testament, Jesus placed the emphasis on eternal salvation. That said, however, Jesus also said God would help those who love him (Matthew 6:24-34) and give us peace (John 16:33). In fact, Jesus even warned his followers about the coming destruction of Jerusalem and how they should flee to the mountains. (Luke 21:20-24)

If Jerusalem was destroyed because the Jews freely chose to hand Jesus over to the Romans to be crucified, then how will it be for Europe and the United States as they, in perfect freedom, forsake

Jesus? Is the coronavirus a divine wakeup call and shot across the bow?

In many ways Europe has paid dearly for its sins inside and outside the Church with wars, plagues and two world wars. During World War I, an angel and later our Blessed Mother, appeared to three shepherd children in Fatima, Portugal when many Portuguese men were away fighting. I mentioned this miraculous event earlier.[34]

In the beginning, an angel appeared to the children on three separate occasions. In the first appearance, the angel said, "Do not be afraid. I am the Angel of Peace. Pray with me." Then he taught the children to pray for those who do not believe, nor adore, nor hope, nor love God.

In the second appearance, the angel told the children to make sacrifices in reparation for sins and for the conversion of sinners. In this way they will draw down peace upon their country. Think about this – the prayers and sacrifices of three young children will bring peace to their country.

In the third visit, the angel gave them holy communion and taught them to pray again for the conversion of sinners and to make amends for the outrages, sacrileges and indifference that offends God. They prayed by offering the presence of Christ in all the tabernacles of the world, i.e., his Body, Blood, Soul and Divinity.

After the angel had prepared the children, our Blessed Mother appeared to them on the 13th day for six months. Our Lady's first words to the children were, "Do not be afraid. I will do you no harm." Then she told them to offer sacrifices and prayers for the conversion of sinners. In the next month, she told them to pray the Rosary every day to bring peace to the world and an end to the war.

---

[34] Fatima for Today, 2012, Father Andrew Apostoli

This time, the children's prayers will bring peace to the world.

In July, our Blessed Mother showed the children a vision of hell. Think about this too -- many grownups today cannot even consider its possibility never mind look at it. Then she said to the children,

> "You have seen hell where the souls of poor sinners go. To save them, God wishes to establish in the world devotion to my Immaculate Heart. If what I say to you is done, many souls will be saved ***and*** there will be peace. [This] war is going to end; but if people do not cease offending God, then a worse [world war] will break out..."

During World War II, at just one Catholic Church in Boston, Our Lady of Perpetual Help on Mission Hill, more than twenty thousand people attended each week to pray for their loved ones and an end to the war. If this were to happen today, or if a truly devastating pandemic spread across the world, how many people would know enough to go to church or attend online faith groups and pray?

As children's prayers contributed to the end of World War I, and as Abraham interceded before God for Sodom and Gomorrah, "What if there are 10 good people there?" (Genesis 18:23-33), so too faithful Catholics can intercede for the world, their loved ones, and themselves.

Some will look askance at visions and apparitions given to the saints, and dismiss them as "private revelations" even though they were approved by the Church. But if God is sending us approved messages, then it only makes sense to pay attention, because these messages simply underscore God's words. For instance, don't the Gospels repeatedly call us to repent, turn away from sin, believe, and receive God's mercy so we may be saved? Aren't all our Saints' approved apparitions mostly repeating the same thing?

Let me be extra clear here. If we in the first world, and especially the United States, continue to walk away from Christ, then I expect God, following the biblical pattern, will remove His protection. Consequently, we will become more vulnerable to pandemics, terrorism, financial collapse, natural disaster, wars, and so forth.

We should consider a lesson from the Roman destruction of Jerusalem. In 66 AD, Roman abuses became too much to take, so the Jews rioted and defeated the local Roman garrison. Rome responded by sending a larger force of soldiers under the command of Gallus. But the Jews routed them as well. This made the Jewish people overconfident thinking they could repel any Roman army. Later, during the feast of Passover when many Jews from surrounding areas entered Jerusalem, a greatly larger Roman army laid siege to the city until it was finally destroyed.

We live in a similar time where we are overconfident in our ability to fight disease, win wars and live prosperously. We don't need or want God's help. When New York's coronavirus numbers started declining, Governor Cuomo said, "The number is down because we brought the number down. God did not do that. Faith did not do that. Our behavior has stopped the spread of the virus. God did not stop the spread of the virus." This is the same governor who a year earlier celebrated the protection and expansion of abortion rights for the full nine months in his state by ordering certain buildings and bridges to be lit pink.

At some point, following biblical patterns, God is going to step back and allow us to be taught a very hard lesson. Given my age, I'm hoping to miss it, though I doubt my children and grandchildren will be so fortunate. Truth is, I just may not miss it either. This will come to pass because we have turned our backs on God and his beloved son unless we start believing and taking our faith seriously.

Where Do We Go from Here?

So here we are with our loved ones on the conveyor belt of this short life, and in light of the crucifixion, we have to decide, is Jesus really who he said he was, son of the living God who came to offer us true love and life while saving us from evil, sin and eternal torment? And is the Catholic Church the **one** church he established to guide, nourish, and inspire us along the way?

My heart goes out to everyone missing life in our Church. The Church is our mother, which my wife is fond of saying, who cares for us through the power of God. This journey is not easy without our Lord's help.

Conversations with Loved Ones

If we take our Lord's words about salvation seriously, then we must go forth outside church walls and have patient caring conversations with those we love. Saint Peter said we must always be ready to explain our hope with gentleness and reverence. (cf. 1 Peter 3:15)

I pray the content of this book, plus other sources you have, will help you initiate and continue these conversations. For me, what is most striking about our faith is not a particular explanation about this or that, but how all Church knowledge fits together with what we know about life, like pieces in a puzzle.

When I'm meeting with parents and godparents preparing to have their children baptized, or with engaged couples getting ready for marriage, I like to have a faith conversation with them rather than make them listen to a lecture. Of course, my ultimate goal is to get them to practice the faith. However, this is probably not going to happen in just one meeting. Rather, in the course of their lives, hopefully many people will encourage them along the Catholic path.

During these meetings, after the welcome, prayer and introductions, I start asking a series of questions to get a sense of where they're at. Depending on their response, I will offer a little perspective similar to what I have done in this book. Keep in mind, however, I'm in an average parish where most people coming in have various doubts and disbelief while also lacking knowledge and experience of the faith. So, in less than an hour, I'm going to try and get them to consider that Jesus Christ and his Church might be true. I will also try to get them to be concerned about standing before God, the father of Jesus crucified, and not to be presumptuous. In a relatively safe and prosperous country, some people need a little healthy fear of the Lord.

I start these sessions with questions like:

- Do you believe in God? (hint: Big Bang)
- Why did God make us? (hint: to love selflessly like God)
- Do you think hell exists and people are actually sent there? (hint: do predators get to live in heaven next door to their victims?)
- Why is there evil? (hint: true love must be freely chosen)

Given the trajectory of our times and decline of the Church, I tell parents and engaged couples that if they want their children to practice the faith, they will have to be very intentional about passing it on to them, because they will possibly not have many friends who are Catholic.

At a Baptism session, I describe how the ritual anticipates the child's entire life since the symbols used correspond to the funeral Mass, for example, the holy water, white pall, and Easter candle. Then I add that the angels and saints in heaven are sitting on the edge of their seats wondering, "Will this child grow up to love God and neighbor more than himself?"

If I were initiating a conversation with a grown child or sibling, we would sit down, and I would ask: What do you believe? What do you believe happens when we die? Do you believe in God? And so forth.

If the response is something like, "I don't believe and I really don't care to think about it," then I'd pull out a palm-size wooden crucifix and say, "Suppose it's really true that God the Father sent us his only beloved son knowing full well he would be crucified, but we could care less. What will it be like when we die and have to stand before Jesus' Father. How will his Father treat us?"

Incidentally, you could also refer him to the other version this book at ItMakesSenseToBelieve.com,[35] then add, "This book will take just a few hours to read or listen to, the amount of time Jesus hung nailed to a cross."

If my loved one still doesn't care to discuss, then so be it for now. Without burning any bridges, though, I would continue to pray and look for ways to help him get closer Jesus and his Church. That said, I would also display the crucifix again and again.

We should always feel secure in our conversations, because the truth is on our side. Whatever questions arise, the Church or intellectually gifted Catholics have already thought through it. We only have to look it up.

Our conversations are not contests that we have to win today, but rather we are patiently journeying with loved ones, supporting them as we grow in knowledge and love of God. The Holy Spirit is orchestrating the help needed for every person. In a lifetime, people we care about will be touched by many persons sent by God.

---

[35] It Makes Sense to Believe at https://www.ItMakesSenseToBelieve.com

There are various benefits to being a practicing Catholic such as growing in love, patience and forgiveness; having the courage and strength to endure tragedy; and finally being prepared to stand before God. Hopefully, those we care about will come to realize this.

Evangelization

The Mormons send out pairs of missionaries to knock on the doors of many homes with whom they have no previous relationship. That's a lot of time-consuming work for an extremely low success rate. Similarly, spending money on commercials and direct-mail campaigns will probably be expensive for a small return.

However, getting our parishioners to care about salvation; then convincing them that our faith is really true; and finally equipping them to have faith conversations with loved ones, will cost almost nothing, take little time, and yield significant fruit for the Church. That said, though, since loved ones often do not reside in the same parish, the parish itself might not benefit much. But if all parishes took this on, then all would benefit. We could start a contra-pandemic to spread the grace of Christ and rebuild his Church.

Preaching & Teaching

Raising the issue of salvation, and sharing reasons why we believe our faith is true, needs to permeate all of our preaching, teaching and Church programs. This is especially important when many of the congregants do not practice their faith regularly.

At most baptisms, weddings and funerals, I estimate 80 to 98 percent of the people in front of me do not practice the faith. I also suppose they lack understanding and are burdened by doubt and disbelief — like most Catholics. Now if I just give an enjoyable feel-good homily, as most expect, then people will leave intuitively surmising they're OK even though they are neglecting and forgetting Jesus. They will never be warned that they are speeding in the dark toward a bridge with a big hole in it.

Except in the situation of a particularly tragic funeral, such as that of a child, I typically segue into a short case for our faith as well as our need to be prepared to stand before God the Father. I will also briefly address some common doubts. In a short homily, it can't be comprehensive, but it's enough to put people on notice, like briefly holding up a lit warning sign.

Now, if you agree with me on equipping parishioners to have faith conversations with loved ones in light of the crucifix, but when those they care about come to our church services and we just happily pat them on the back, then we are effectively undermining those conversations because they've never heard concern from church clergy. However, if we uphold those discussions in every service, then over time, people will start to reconsider.

Admittedly, this is a difficult homily to prepare and deliver, because we have to take folks from where they are and what they expect, to what we want them to hear, so they might reconsider Jesus and be confidently saved. In our lives, most of us have had to initiate uncomfortable conversations that might generate negative feelings. Or have had to endure someone raising a sensitive topic. This must happen in relationships that are caring and honest. Likewise, homilies that will disturb, such as on salvation, must be preached. Other opportunities for this type of homily include Christmas Eve, Easter, Ash Wednesday, and training the parents of students in faith formation.

A few months after I was ordained, my mother passed away. Hers was my first funeral Mass as a deacon. Since some of my beloved family members did not practice the faith, I prepared a somewhat intense and challenging homily. What I didn't expect before Mass, as I walked down the center aisle to the back of the church, was that my boss from work and Jewish colleague were there. But I stayed the course and delivered my prepared sermon.

When I went to work the next morning and entered my cube opposite my boss' office, she was already there and immediately called me in. I sat down and she said, "You know my youngest is almost out of high school. We're done with youth sports. I could go back to Mass." I smiled and told her I didn't know she was Catholic until I gave her Communion.

During Sunday homilies we need to touch upon common issues and doubts, like sex, gender, reliability of Scripture and Church teaching, caring for those in need, and so forth. Again, on every topic we must try to take folks from what they believe to what the Church believes, giving them good common-sense explanations and divine insights. People need to see that our faith makes sense. Eventually, they will start to believe and trust.

Vocations to Priesthood and Religious Life

When my oldest sons were 11 and 12, I went to confession and told the priest how aggravated I got when they neglected responsibilities and fooled around. Sensing my displeasure with the boys, the priest replied, "The biggest sacrifice I made in becoming a priest was not being able to have my own children." That really stayed with me on a couple of levels. The obvious was I should be grateful to God for blessing us with wonderful sons. Later, I started to think about the sacrifices some priests must make, such as, not being able to have a wife and children.

Now if we believe just about everyone goes to heaven, whether or not they practice the faith and get closer to Jesus, then a man will become a priest because he likes the vocation and lifestyle; it suits his relationship with God; and, he would like to share the joy he receives with others. But he will probably not give up something else he would most prefer to do, like getting married and having children.

On the other hand, if a man believes people's salvation is at risk, and they need instruction and sacraments to be ensured of eternal life, then he will sacrifice anything out of his love for God and neighbor.

When I graduated college in 1978, I was very inspired by Saint Francis of Assisi and decided to enter the seminary to become a priest in the foreign missions. With my simple faith, I thought it was the best way to serve God.

But I was naive and lacked a lot of Catholic knowledge when I started formation. I didn't realize until 15 years later, when I began reading the new Catechism and listening to instruction on EWTN, that I was not taught in the seminary what the Church officially believes. For instance, after almost 18 months in the seminary, I met with a panel of three priests who were going to rubber stamp me onto the next semester. To their surprise, I told them we needed to talk; explained that I entered the seminary for the wrong reasons; and that I didn't know why we needed priests. About my reasoning and last point, they had no response.

Three years later, I met my wife to be, while we were in the School of Social Work. In terms of looks, intelligence, work ethic, and professional polish, she was a solid grade above me. If I were a B, she was a solid A. Interestingly, she was drawn to me because I loved God.

At the time of this writing, my wife and I have three terrific grown sons, a wonderful daughter-in-law, and two beautiful granddaughters. Yet, even with such a blessed family and knowing what I know now, if I were making the vocation decision again at 23 years old, I would choose to become to a priest.

Yes, I would not have a family out of a passion to save souls. I say this even though the only period I was ever lonely in my entire life, was when I was in the seminary.

Now you might think I wish I were a priest today, but you would misunderstand my point. I visited eight religious orders before entering the seminary. If God wanted me to become a priest, he would have placed me in an order that was faithful to Church understanding. Rather, because I was open-minded to God's will, I believe God put me exactly where he wants me. And I'm very happy he did. In fact, the irony is, I live in mission territory now.

If we take the issue of salvation, sin, and divine forgiveness seriously, then we need many more priests to hear confessions and anoint the dying. And if the coronavirus reduces the number of people that can attend Mass at one time, then we might need more Masses and also more priests.

As for religious sisters and brothers, we need their faith-filled vocations to, for instance, affordably form Catholic children in schools and care for the elderly in nursing homes. Today, children are being poorly directed by our culture and the demise of old folks is being hastened by some heartless caregivers. Historically, religious orders have generously responded to the physical and spiritual needs of God's people, especially the poor and vulnerable.

About the discipline of celibacy, I think the Church will get much more flexible service from celibate vocations than married ministers, as Jesus said, some will renounce marriage for the sake of the kingdom (Matthew 19:12b) This is a practical reality. Even if both spouses were passionately committed to serving our Lord, they still need time together, must raise children, and cannot be sent to separate parts of the world. The Church will probably get more from a celibate man and woman, than a married couple. For instance, if Saints Pope John Paul II and Mother Teresa were first married to each other, I doubt they would have accomplished so much for the kingdom.

Moreover, if a person really wants to serve the Lord, he risks not being able to do so if he gets married. For instance, desired ministry positions that pay enough to support a family might be difficult to find. Also, the ongoing support of one's spouse is not guaranteed, but could diminish in time as both deal with life's challenges, and as their faith ebbs and flows.

I suspect God has called many handsome young adults to Church vocations, but they had a greater desire to be married first, and to minister second. I say this not to judge those already married, but to challenge those who are not, so they might more intentionally consider giving up family to more completely serve God and save souls. But let me also add, I think married life and raising godly children (Malachi 2:15), can be the most difficult of all vocations.

Forgiveness

I have probably emphasized enough our need to periodically go to a priest, receive the Sacrament of Confession, and in fact be forgiven by God for our sins. But if this has not been done in years, then I encourage you to make an appointment right away.

When I started studying Scripture and the Church Catechism in earnest, I noticed I had a lot to confess. However, I wanted this to be a "good" confession. So, I set up an appointment with the most serious priest in the area I knew; I didn't want to get off quickly and easily. As I confessed my sins, I found the priest to be very nice. He tried to interrupt me, feeling I was being too hard on myself. I replied, "Father, I know what I'm doing." And he let me finish.

While being forgiven by God is an uplifting experience, we also need to be merciful – to ourselves, others, and sometimes God.

When we receive God's mercy, then we need to forgive ourselves. It's OK to hold on to a tinge of guilt, so we don't repeat our mistakes. But we must deeply feel our heavenly Father's overwhelming and enthusiastic love for us. As Jesus said, "There will be more rejoicing in heaven over one repentant sinner, than ninety-nine who have no need to repent." (Luke 15:7)

Remember the story of the Prodigal Son. How when the son was returning home, his father saw him a great distance away, and ran to him. Before his son could apologize, his father embraced and kissed him. Then he barely spoke his words of apology before his father commanded his servants to dress him in the best robe; put shoes on his feet and a ring on his finger; and kill the fatted calf for a big party and celebration. (Luke 15:11-24) This is how Jesus portrayed our heavenly Father.

Remember as well how Jesus during his crucifixion prayed to God saying, "Father, forgive them for they don't know what they are doing." (Luke 23:34) Then one of the criminals crucified beside Jesus acknowledged that his sentence fit the crime and asked Jesus to remember him when he comes into his kingdom. Jesus replied, "Today, you will be with me in paradise." (Luke 23:32-43)

So, we must always keep in mind how rich in mercy God is and how anxious he is to forgive us, if we will only return to him. After that, we need to forgive ourselves.

It's important to note, too, there is a kind of benefit to having sinned, not that there is ever any valid reason to do so on purpose. When we acknowledge our sins in confession, we become more humble. This in turn makes us more tolerant and forgiving of those who have wronged us. And it is critical that we do.

In the prayer Jesus taught, he said, "Pray to our Father... forgive us our trespasses as we forgive those who trespass against us." Then Jesus added, "if you do not forgive others, neither will your Father forgive the things you have done wrong." (Matthew 6:9-15)

This is so important to understand. If we are intolerant of other people's mistakes and hold grudges, how will it be when we get to the door of heaven and want to enter, but the person we resent is already in heaven? Don't we realize that everyone in heaven is in intimate communion with each other? That he will be in me and I will be in him? Please be clear, we cannot enter heaven until we have forgiven. There might be a lot of people spending long stretches of time in purgatory for this reason.

Lacking forgiveness is an enormous problem for human beings. It breaks up relationships and families; perpetuates strife between nations and peoples; and is like cancer in the soul for the one who cannot forgive.

Finally, since life can be extremely difficult and unfair, we might even have to forgive God. Because this is how he loves us, when we are unfair to him; and, of course, we must learn to love like God.

Conclusion

This is a difficult time to pass the faith onto those we love. The biggest reason why people today are leaving Catholicism, or are not coming to church, or are lukewarm at Mass, is they doubt and disbelieve Church teaching. And many of those we love are affected by this. Consequently, I have tried to present a case that relies on evidence and common sense to demonstrate why it is so certain that God exists; Jesus is his only beloved son; and he established one Church to guide and nourish us.

But even if this book were a great case, it would still be a challenge to get those we love to take time to consider it because they do not need God in this life and expect eternal life. This presumption, however, is not supported by Jesus' words.

As a deacon during Mass, when I look at all the empty seats in front of me, I know there are many baptized Catholics in town not coming to worship. I worry for them and their children standing before God, the father of Jesus crucified, having neglected and forgotten his beloved son. Not only that, as our Church declines, I have increasing concern for the safety of our world and its temporal happiness.

Therefore, we must start having conversations with loved ones. At some point I suggest putting a modest crucifix in front of them and asking, "Should we take a little time to consider if Jesus was truly sent by God to save us from sin and for divine love? Or when our life ends, as it will one day, should we just take our chances?"

To help this conversation, the case in this book presented three reasons for believing God most likely exists, and twelve more for believing in Jesus Christ and the one Church he established, despite a multitude of faith alternatives. The fact that the Catholic faith fits so well with what we know about life, like pieces in a puzzle, is very compelling. All other options require blind faith or leaps that defy evidence and reason.

To further aid the discussion, and with this case as context, we considered well known controversies, such as, horrific scandals, sexual morality, and women's ordination. These are prominent and important issues. But we cannot reject such a compelling faith over this or that problem, especially if we have not investigated the Church's inspiration on it. And if we do not choose the Catholic Church, then where else will we go?

Even though I am concerned for many people, I cannot completely blame them for falling away from the Church. In my experience, many Catholic teachers and preachers, while being very caring and committed, did a poor job promoting all God's words and invisible realities; teaching people to resolve doubts and disbeliefs; and helping them work out their salvation. In the Great Commission (Matthew 28:18-20), Jesus did not tell his disciples to go out to the whole world and primarily show them how nice, friendly, and welcoming we are. Rather, he told them to baptize and make disciples of all the nations, teaching them *all* that he commanded.

When clergy were first ordained to the diaconate, each one knelt before the bishop who handed him a Book of the Gospels and said, "Receive the Gospel of Christ whose herald you have become. *Believe what you read*, teach what you believe, and practice what you teach." Unfortunately, promoting the entire Gospel was not widely done in my time and many of our local churches have dwindled as a result. We did not believe all of Jesus' words, and we did not let the weightiness of all his words sink into our souls. No, it was more like the Parable of the Sower (Matthew 13), where some of the words sunk in, but others did not. And sadly, the problem continues to this day.

When those we care about, see us disbelieve various words of the Church and Scripture, then they will feel they can pick and choose as well. Consequently, doubt and disbelief will grow like cancer, and people will fall way. However, to the extent all Church members uphold our entire faith, then many will start to listen. Therefore, it is up to the ordained, religious and lay faithful who believe all God's words to reach out and help their relatives and friends embrace the Church.

In the old days, it seemed effortless for parents to pass the faith to their children, like it was a lit torch or candle, because the culture was predominantly Catholic and Protestant. Today, in a secular environment, those with faith must deliberately put it onto the minds and hearts of those they love.

Jesus once wondered, "When the Son of Man returns, will he find faith on earth?" (Luke 18:8) When I was a child, people would have thought this was a silly question. But given the demise of the Church in only my lifetime, Jesus' question might be prophetic. It is up to every Catholic who cares about his Church and preparing loved ones to face God, to pray in earnest and initiate conversations that will bring them back to the faith.

Resources for Loved Ones

There is a world full of terrific Catholic resources. But these are what have been most valuable to me.

Bible

At the very least we should get to know at least one Gospel very well. There are four Gospels, about 30 pages each, that recount the life of Jesus.

The Revised Standard Version, Catholic Edition (RSV-CE)

Used by the Catechism with special editions published by Ignatius Press, Ascension Press, and the Midwest Theological Forum.

The New American Bible, Revised Edition (NABRE)

Used at Mass. Available at Catholic bookstores.

Bible Gateway for Online Search

Can search against one or more Bible versions at the same time. https://www.biblegateway.com/keyword/

Catechism of the Catholic Church

This is the first, official universal catechism of the Church since the Council of Trent centuries ago. It was published in the 1990s and is rich in references to Sacred Scripture, Church documents and writings of Saints going back to the beginning.

Catechism of the Catholic Church, Second Edition

Available from Ignatius Press.

The Spiritual Life

The Fulfillment of All Desire, by Ralph Martin, 2006

Professor Martin systematically presents insights from seven spiritual doctors of the Church to help guide us into having a personal relationship with Jesus Christ. This book is also available on Amazon and Audible.

Learning the Bible

A Father Who Keeps His Promises, by Scott Hahn, 1998

This brief, very accessible book helped me immediately begin to understand the Bible. This is a byproduct of Professor Hahn's doctoral thesis on salvation history. Available at DynamicCatholic.com and Audible Books.

The Bible Timeline: The Story of Salvation

This was called The Big Picture. It's an in-depth video study of biblical history. In a sense, it expands on Scott Hahn's book. This is available at Ascension Press along with many other quality study programs.

These two sources provide the context so you can deep-dive and study any book in the Bible.

Catholic Publishers

Ascension Press (https://ascensionpress.com)

A great collection of video and online study programs, as well as books, etc.

Ignatius Press (https://www.ignatius.com)

Has just about everything.

2 Great True Stories

Both these stories are fun, contemporary reads that show the power of prayer, and are examples of how God works tangibly in people's lives.

Mother Angelica: The Remarkable Story of a Nun, Her Nerve, and a Network of Miracles, by Raymond Arroyo, 2007

An extraordinary and hilarious biography of a poor Catholic nun creating the largest religious cable network in the world. Available on Amazon and Audible.

The Shadow of His Wings: The True Story of Fr. Gereon Goldmann, OFM

This is Father Goldmann's exciting autobiography on how he grew up in Germany as a Catholic youth, ended up in Hitler's SS, was ordained a priest during the war, and lived to tell about it. Republished by Ignatius Press in 2000. Available on Amazon.

Subscription Resources

Magnificat (https://us.magnificat.net/)

Magnificat magazine or its phone app is a great daily resource for prayer. It contains the readings for daily Mass as well as reflections from spiritual writers.

Formed (https://formed.org)

Has a large library of on-demand video lectures and inspirational movies.

Word on Fire (https://wordonfire.org)

Founded by Bishop Robert Barron, this ministry contains a wealth of high-quality formation resources.

Television

CatholicTV (https://catholictv.org)

Incidentally, CatholicTV is located in my hometown of Watertown, MA, behind Saint Patrick's parish where I am a deacon.

Eternal Word Television Network (ETWN – https://ewtn.com)

Founded by Mother Angelica, this is the largest religious cable network organization in the world.

YouTube

Most of my favorite speakers can be found on YouTube. They have also written books and so forth. In no special order they are Ralph Martin, Scott Hahn, Bishop Robert Barron, Deacon Harold Burke-Sivers, Steve Ray, Curtis Martin, Patrick Madrid, Jeff Cavins, Father Mike Schmitz, Father John Riccardo, Jennifer Fulwiler, Johnnette Benkovic, Janet Smith... To explore long list of Catholic speakers, see this page: https://www.lighthousecatholicmedia.org/store/speakers.

Questions?

Catholic Answers (https://www.catholic.com/)

Catholic Answers is my go-to website whenever I want a clear concise answer to a question.

The Coming Home Network (https://chnetwork.org/)

Many protestant ministers and leaders from other faiths have studied their way into the Catholic Church when pursuing truth. This organization has been a great help to them. Also, the testimonies of these religious leaders are inspirational.

Made in the USA
Middletown, DE
03 February 2021